10 minute facelift

10 minute
facelift

rejuvenate your face
the natural way

Jennie Harding

p

This is a Parragon Publishing Book
This edition published in 2006

Parragon Publishing
Queen Street House
4 Queen Street
Bath BA1 1HE, UK

Copyright © Parragon Books Ltd 2005

ISBN: 1-40545-588-8

Printed in China

Created and produced by
THE BRIDGEWATER BOOK COMPANY

studio photography Ian Parsons
model Kate Lincoln

contents

introduction
what is a facelift?

The face is one of our most powerful cultural images, and has been for thousands of years. Temple paintings and masterpieces in oils have, over the centuries, given way to movie, television, and magazine images of faces airbrushed or digitally altered to perfection. The quest to create and maintain a flawless face fuels a massive global cosmetics industry; yet even the countless lotions and potions on sale cannot halt the inevitable onslaught of time. More direct ways to slow the aging process may be required.

Even a perfectly healthy complexion shows subtle changes as the face ages over time

A facelift is technically a procedure that is designed to restructure the face, which includes the bones, muscles, and ligaments, as well as to tighten slack skin. This procedure is mostly achieved through surgical intervention. For some people, cosmetic surgery is actually necessary, for example to rehabilitate someone after an accident, but these days more and more people are seeking it out deliberately to repair what they see in themselves as unattractive, or to combat the process of aging. A surgical facelift can, however, be very expensive and recovery may take some time.

Does a facelift have to be such a dramatic intervention? Perhaps not: it depends on how you define it and what you want to achieve. Using specific exercises and techniques, it is perfectly possible to achieve a high level of facial toning, which supports the muscles and keeps the skin looking and feeling supple. The sooner these techniques are practiced and the longer they are used, the better the results over time. These techniques are based on natural therapies—including massage, pressure points, energetic techniques, and aromatherapy—that have been used for centuries to promote and maintain facial tone and a youthful complexion.

This book will show you how to use a wide variety of tools to achieve what we will call facial rejuvenation. By following these techniques you cannot restructure your face in a surgical way, but you will find out how to create a huge variety of fun 10-minute routines that can easily be incorporated into your daily life and can make a real difference to the shape and tone of your face. You will discover many different ways to give yourself a face massage, how to use facial exercises, how to blend essential oils to support muscle and skin tone for your individual skin type, and how to give yourself treatments that are the equivalent of a professional facial.

This book also takes a look at beauty on a much deeper level—not just what is visible on the outside, but also what is going on under the skin. Find out how to feed your muscles and skin with super nutrients, how to ensure elasticity, how to clean away toxins, and how to get the best-quality sleep to nourish not just your face but also your whole being. Beauty is not just skin deep: our faces reflect our feelings, moods, and emotions. Discover how to make a vibrant new routine for yourself.

a close look
at the face

In this chapter, we will take an in-depth look at the face, from the bony structure of the skull, through the muscles to the upper layers of the skin. You will have the chance to assess your skin type, which will then help you to know how to care for it. We look at the causes of facial aging, such as sunlight and poor diet, and assess what you can do to minimize their effects. Finally, you are encouraged to analyze your own face, using Eastern face diagnosis, in order to help correct any energetic imbalances.

1

the face from the inside out

The structure of the face involves bones, muscles, and the skin that covers these areas. Facial rejuvenation techniques work on the muscles and skin to achieve tightening and toning effects. Try touching your face with your fingers to feel these structures for yourself.

bones

The face forms the front of the skull and is made up of 13 bones in total. There are two cheekbones, which create the shape of the face. The upper jaw area is made up of two bones, which are fused below the nose. The lower jaw is movable when we talk or chew, thanks to the temporo-mandibular joints just under the ears. The nose is made up of two flat bones, which join in the middle. The forehead is part of the dome of the skull, called the frontal bone.

muscles

Important facial muscles connect to the bony structure; they enable the eyes to open, the eyebrows to lift, and the mouth to chew. Notice the big muscles in the cheek (the masseters), the ring of muscle around each eye area (the orbicularis oculi), the temporalis muscles on either side of the head, which actually assist in chewing, and the circle of muscle around the mouth (the orbicularis). Slack muscle tone in these areas directly affects facial shape, and so these will be exercised, massaged, or worked using pressure points in your facelift routines.

skin

This tissue covers the whole body, regulating temperature through sweat glands and providing contact with the world via countless nerve endings. The skin on the face is more delicate than elsewhere on the body, because the muscle layer underneath is less dense. The skin, which rests on a bed of insulating subcutaneous fat, comprises two layers: the dermis, which contains important blood vessels, nerve endings, hair follicles, and special glands that secrete the skin's own lubricating oils, and the epidermis, which is made up of overlapping skin cells that are constantly rubbed away and replaced. This process of renewal slows with time, so facial rejuvenation techniques are needed to nourish and replenish this layer. As you will see, there are different skin types, classified by their relative oiliness or dryness. It's important to choose the right methods and ingredients to treat your individual needs.

the main skin types

Facelift techniques work on muscles that lie under the skin, but the surface needs attention as well. There are several different skin types, and this guide should help you to identify your own needs. Once you recognize your complexion, you will be able to choose skin-enhancing routines to revitalize your face as part of your individual facelift treatment plan.

normal

This soft-textured, well-hydrated, supple skin has a healthy glow and no visible wrinkles, lines, or large pores.

dry

This very fine-textured and velvety skin has an almost "stretched" look and a tendency to become red very quickly in sun or wind.

oily

The oil glands in this skin are overactive, producing very shiny skin with large open pores and a coarse texture all over; it is often accompanied by oily hair.

mature

This skin type is showing the effects of aging: it is losing elasticity and sagging, with a dull texture and deepening

lines or wrinkles, or areas of irregular pigmentation, such as liver spots or moles.

combination

This skin type often shows a T-zone of oiliness over the forehead, nose, and chin, with dry areas on the cheeks. It is very common in puberty but can also be found in adults.

sensitive

This allergy-prone skin tends to break out in rashes, sometimes accompanied by itching or burning sensations; it is often sensitive to cosmetics.

blemish-prone

Acne and blackheads are most often found in oily areas, and flare-ups of the condition may occur because of hormonal fluctuations. Blemish-prone skins can also be sensitive.

Your cultural heritage can also affect your skin type. Darker skins are often naturally supple and well lubricated, so they require lighter-textured massage oils or creams. By contrast, lighter-shaded complexions have more of a tendency to dryness and may well require treatment products with a richer base.

Comparing young and more mature skin shows you what happens to the complexion over time. Notice the even, supple tone of a young face, and then the changes in a mature person—loss of tone, elasticity, and healthy glow… But don't worry—this book will teach you how to slow down this process! With the right tools, you can make a real difference to your face.

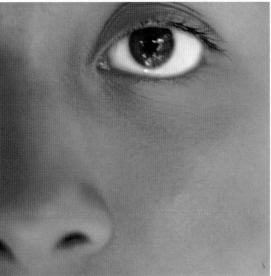

why does the face age?

The first thing to realize is that we are all "aging" from the moment we are born, and so the signs of aging are just part of a natural process. This constant change that we see reflected in the mirror is, however, affected by certain factors, some of which we can influence positively through lifestyle awareness.

sunlight

Overexposure to high levels of intense sunlight is extremely damaging to lighter complexions, causing burning and even skin cancer; darker skins contain much higher levels of pigment to protect them. Mild exposure to sunlight in your home environment as the seasons change is beneficial—after all, the body needs sunlight to manufacture vitamin D, which is vital for bone health. However, if you are going on vacation to a hot climate, it is vital to use adequate sun protection, especially on the delicate skin of your face.

poor diet

Many people nowadays consume a diet that contains many lowfat products, unaware that we may be depriving our body of some of the fats it really needs. Saturated fats, such as those found in red meat, are not good for general health if consumed to excess, but unsaturated fats, such as those found in olive oil, are not only beneficial to our health but are also known to improve the texture and suppleness of skin and hair. Your diet should therefore include minimum amounts of saturated fats and higher amounts of unsaturated fats.

Processed foods, such as potato chips and cookies, are frequently high in salt and sugar and so are unlikely to have much nutritional value for the skin. They should therefore be avoided. By contrast, fresh fruit and vegetables are vital to good skin health and so should be eaten freely.

stress and sleeplessness

During quality sleep, fresh blood supply nourishes the skin, removing toxins and supplying nutrients. If there are emotional stresses, these can interfere with sleep patterns, creating a tired and dull complexion. In addition, unconscious reactions to stress can cause facial expressions such as frowning or teeth clenching.

poor muscle tone

Slack face muscles are actually very common, and often occur simply because we don't chew our food properly. Chewing not only releases more saliva and helps to improve digestion, but it also exercises the cheek muscles. It is important to include plenty of raw fruit and vegetables in our diet to make sure we do enough chewing to exercise our cheek muscles.

face analysis

Here is a chance to have a good, close-up look at yourself to assess the structure and features of your face. The purpose of this exercise is not to be overly self-critical: you are simply aiming to get a realistic view of what you are working with so that you can decide what help you need to improve your face.

Before starting, remove all your makeup, leaving your skin completely clean, then sit in front of a large mirror with good lighting for a clear view. You may like to make a few notes for yourself.

facial structure

Using your fingertips, feel the shape of your face and its contours. How is the tone of the muscles in your cheeks, chin, and jaw: is it good, medium, or slack?

skin features and tone

Are there any lines or wrinkles on your face? If so, where are they? Are they deep or superficial? Also, what type of skin do you have (see pages 12–13)? Are there any moles, thread veins, or blemishes?

eastern face diagnosis

In traditional Eastern medicine, there are links between features on the face and energy imbalances associated with the different meridians of the body. See if you have any of these signs, and then notice how simple dietary measures can help to remedy them.

SKIN DIAGNOSIS

- Oily skin between the eyebrows
- Deep creases between
  the eyebrows
- Redness/rashes between
  the eyebrows

These are all signs of liver imbalance: increase the levels of leafy green vegetables in your diet.

- Bluish-green bruised-looking areas
  at the base of the nose on the
  sides of the nostrils

These are signs of pancreas imbalance: reduce your refined sugar intake and eat more sweet vegetables such as carrots and pumpkin

- Puffiness below the eyes
- Shadows below the eyes

These are signs of kidney imbalance: reduce the amount of salt in your diet and eat plenty of warm soups/stews.

- Dry, cracked, or puffy
  lower lip

This is a sign of large intestine imbalance: reduce your intake of raw foods and yeast, and increase your intake of rice and cooked root vegetables.

- Spots, broken veins, or rashes on
  the cheeks

These are signs of lung imbalance: reduce your intake of wheat and dairy produce, and eat more spices, like ginger, for example.

Note: these signs are not indicative of diseases in any of the organs mentioned; they simply point to aspects of the body's energy that need correcting.

beauty from within

To make the most of your features, it is really important to keep the muscles of the face toned and supple. This chapter is full of exercises and other techniques that will make a real difference to your face over time. Each routine takes only 10 minutes, so have fun trying them out, and then select the ones that work best for your face. You can also target potential problem areas, such as the chin or cheeks, with special exercises. If you practice your routines regularly, you will see a real difference in your face.

2

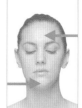

simple face exercises
to tone and uplift

Facial exercises stretch, move, and tone the face muscles much more specifically than speaking and eating. After this routine you may be surprised at how much you can "feel" the muscles—especially since you are barely aware of them most of the time. If you have never done exercises like this before, start gently and increase gradually.

For this exercise routine, make sure you wear comfortable clothes and have your hair tidy. Your face should be cleansed and moisturized. Start slowly and gently to warm up, and relax afterward by taking a few deep breaths.

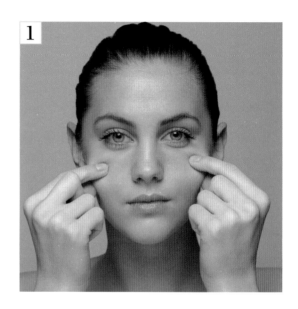

1 Using your thumb and index finger together, gently pick up folds of skin all over your face, and gently squeeze then release them. This exercise stimulates the circulation and wakes up the face. Continue for 1 minute.

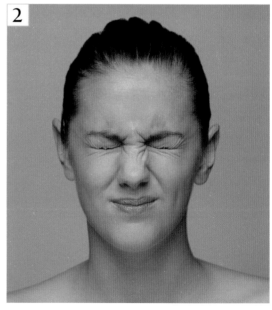

2 Make a really screwed-up face, hold it for 3 seconds, then slowly release your muscles. Repeat this exercise three times. This move tenses and relaxes all the facial muscles and works on areas that may not normally be well exercised.

3 With your mouth closed, pretend you are chewing something. Notice the direction in which you chew naturally, and do this exercise for about half a minute; then try to chew the other way. Don't overdo this movement, just chew slowly for about 1 minute in total. This exercise stretches the muscles of the jaw area and also the chin.

4 Stick your tongue out and try to touch the tip of your nose. Don't force this movement: go only as far as you can, then relax. This movement exercises the muscles under the chin area. Repeat three times.

5 With your lips closed, use your tongue to "brush" your teeth; this action creates a really interesting feeling, because the tongue is so sensitive. As well as increasing the production of saliva in your mouth, the movement of your tongue exercises muscles in the cheeks and chin. Continue for about 1 minute.

6 Rub your hands together briskly, then place them over your face and feel the warmth beneath them. Breathe deeply several times.

6
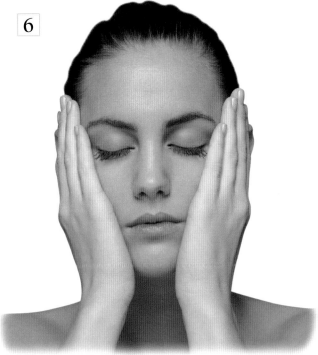

4
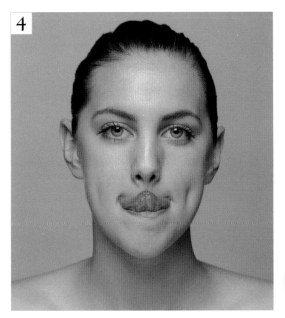

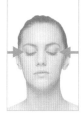

yoga exercises
for the eyes

In yogic tradition, the eyes are exercised in various ways not only to improve vision but also to tone the eye muscles, which helps to improve circulation to the whole area, including the skin. Start this sequence gently; over time, as the muscles get used to the exercises, you will be able to complete the sequence smoothly.

Sit comfortably on a straight-backed chair, with your legs uncrossed and hands resting lightly in your lap. Keep your chin level and move only your eyes, not your head or neck. Breathe gently and evenly throughout the sequence. Don't strain or force any movements: go only as far as is comfortable. Close your eyes to relax at the end.

tip
This routine really soothes your eyes at the end of the day, particularly if you read a lot or work on a computer. Keeping the eye muscles toned helps to improve circulation to that part of the face.

1

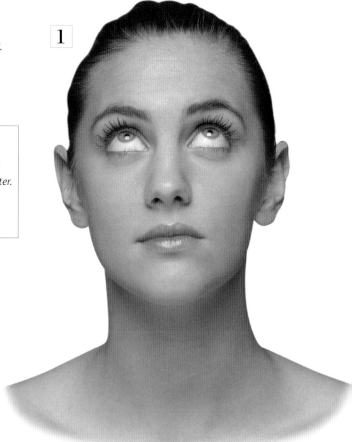

1 Look upward as far as you can, as if you were looking up into your head. Hold for 3 seconds, then release. Repeat three times.

2 Look down as far as you can, as if all the way down to your toes. Hold for 3 seconds, then release. Repeat three times.

3 Look to your right as far as you can, being aware of the edge of your visual field. Hold for 3 seconds, then release. Repeat three times.

4 Repeat step 3, but looking to your left. Hold for 3 seconds, then release. Repeat three times.

5 Starting in step 1 position, move your eyes slowly round to the right, then down, then to the left, and then back to the starting position, in a smooth circular rotation. Take your time. Repeat the sequence again.

6 Now focus both eyes on the tip of your nose, just for a few moments, then release. This exercises eye muscles that are deep in the skull. Repeat twice more.

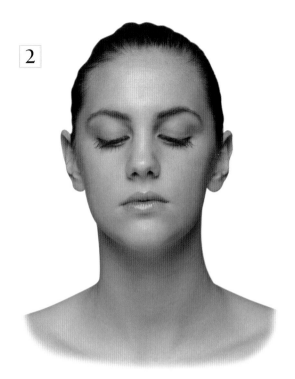

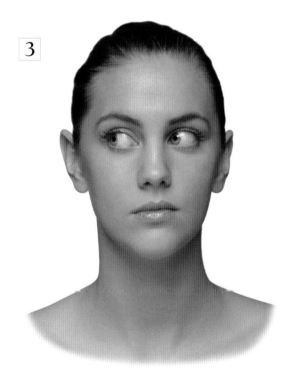

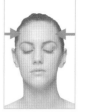

face exercises
for the forehead

The forehead shows not only aging lines but also facial expressions caused by stress, such as frown marks. We often don't realize that our repetitive thoughts and stresses literally make their mark on our faces. The role of the mind in releasing stress is very important, and you should aim to have relaxing thoughts as you work through the exercises.

1

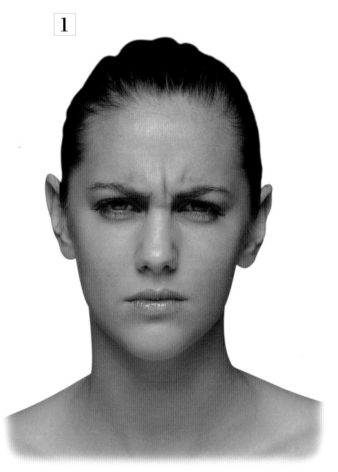

To prepare, sit comfortably on a hard-backed chair, with your legs uncrossed and hands resting lightly in your lap. You may like to play some pleasant music while you work. Breathe easily and regularly throughout the exercise.

1 A short frown can be a good exercise; try it for 3 seconds and then slowly release. Feel the change in your facial muscles. When you are angry or intense, this muscle clenching is what happens to your face. Repeat three times, but without any stress!

2 Using your fingertips, push the skin of your forehead up toward the hairline then down toward the eyebrow line. This exercise feels relaxing to do, and it makes you aware of how thin the layer of skin and muscle is over this bony area. Repeat three times.

3 Place your fingers in your hair and rest the heels of your hands against the hairline. Tense your arms and hands and gently pull toward the back of your head, stretching the skin of the forehead. Hold for a few seconds, then relax. Repeat three times.

4 Place both hands over your forehead with your palms against the skin. Slowly squeeze out toward the sides of the forehead, imagining that you are "wiping away" tension. Repeat three times.

5 Use your fingertips to make tiny circular movements all along the very edge of your hairline. This exercise is amazingly relaxing and improves circulation to the area. It can also ease a headache. Continue for about 1 minute.

6 Close your eyes and focus on your forehead area. How does it feel now? Notice any feelings of tingling or warmth—these are signs of improved circulation and muscle tone.

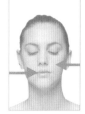

face exercises for the
cheeks and mouth

Signs of aging in the cheeks show up as slack muscles, which cause a drooping effect in the lower jaw area, perhaps with loose folds of skin. One of the best and simplest exercises is to chew some raw food, such as carrot or celery, at least once daily to exercise the muscles in the cheeks and around the mouth.

Sit comfortably in a hard-backed chair, with your legs uncrossed and hands resting lightly in your lap. These exercises use sounds as well as face postures, so you might like to play some music to disguise the sounds you will make!

1 Take a deep breath and, as you exhale, make an exaggerated "aah" shape with your mouth, sounding the vowel at the same time. Do this slowly three times. Feel the muscles in your cheeks begin to stretch.

2 Breathe in, then exhale and make an exaggerated "air" sound, feeling how the shape of your face changes as the vowel changes. Repeat three times.

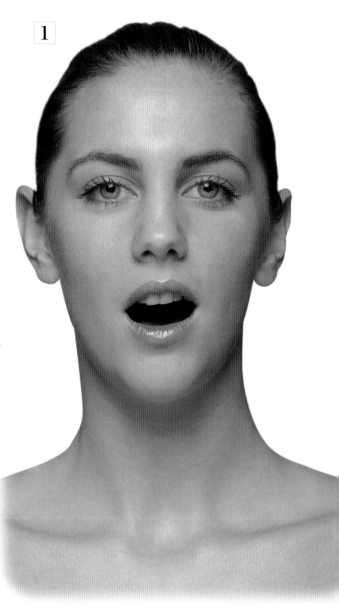

3 Breathe in, then exhale and make an exaggerated "ee" sound. As the sound changes, note that your face is now in a totally different shape and position. Repeat three times.

4 Breathe in, then exhale and make an exaggerated "or" sound; now your mouth is rounded and you can really feel the cheeks working hard. Repeat three times.

5 Breathe in, then exhale and make an exaggerated "oo" sound. This position engages the ring of muscle around the mouth, the cheek area, and the muscles under the chin. Repeat three times.

6 Now slowly form all five sounds in turn—"aah," "air," "ee," "or," "oo"—feeling your face working and changing as the sounds change. Repeat the whole sequence three times. Your face should now feel well exercised.

Doing this exercise makes you aware of how sounds and speech are working the muscles in the cheeks and lower jaw.

4

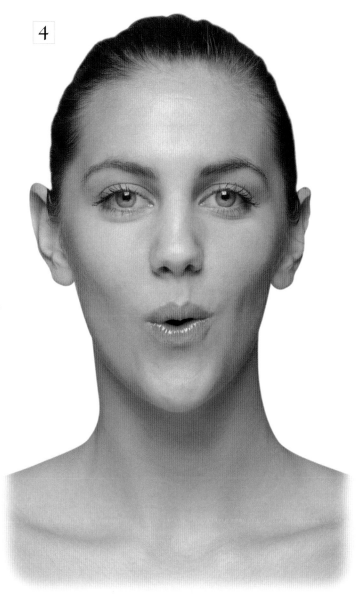

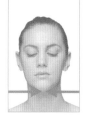

face exercises
for the chin

The chin area is connected to the neck and shoulders by a large area of powerful muscle called the sterno-cleido-mastoid, which allows the head to twist and turn. This extensive flap of muscle anchors in under the clavicle and connects to the chin as far up as behind the ear. The following exercises work this muscle in particular.

neck rolls

Sit comfortably on a stool with your back straight, your feet flat on the floor, and your hands resting in your lap. These movements need to flow into each other, and nothing should be forced. Breathe slowly and regularly as you work.

1 Keeping your back straight and your shoulders still, tilt your head downward, comfortably.

2 Slowly roll your head toward your right shoulder, going only as far as you comfortably can.

3 Now gently tilt your head backward, being careful not to strain your neck, especially if you have problems in this area.

4 Finally, roll your head toward your left shoulder before returning to the starting position to complete the circular movement.

Repeat the sequence once more, slowly, in the same direction, then twice more going in the opposite direction.

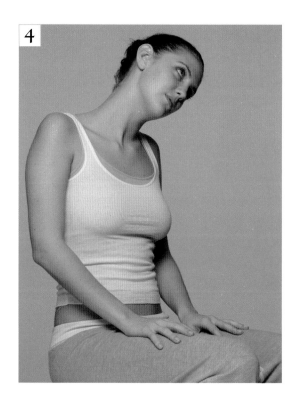

4

yoga lion pose

This pose is a single yoga posture that is quite unusual, and may feel a little strange, but this genuine yoga pose is very effective at waking up the whole system, as well as working chin and neck muscles.

1 Kneel down on the floor and sit on your heels, resting your hands on the edges of your knees, with your palms splayed out in front of you.

2 Breathe in, then, as you exhale, lean forward slightly, stretching your tongue out and down, stretching your fingers out, and focusing your eyes directly upward. Hold this pose for as long as you can, then breathe naturally a few times. Repeat the posture twice more.

As a variation, try making the "aah" sound as you go into this pose with your tongue out. See if this makes the exercise feel different.

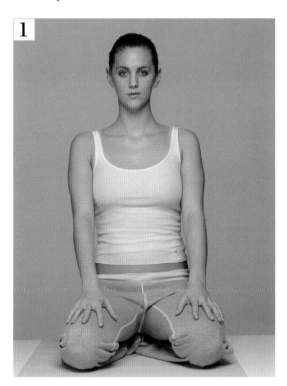

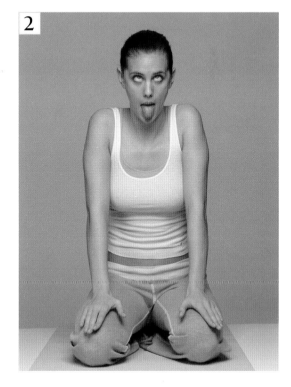

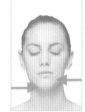

face exercises
for the jaw

Exercises for the jaw involve a very important joint called the temporo-mandibular joint (or TMJ). Some of the most important muscles in the face also connect into this area. Tension in your TMJ can cause toothache or headaches, and working it gently benefits the bony structure of the face as well as the muscles of the jaw.

For this series of exercises, sit in a hard-backed chair, with your legs uncrossed and your back straight. Don't overdo the movements, and if you feel any discomfort, stop straight away.

1 Place your fingers under your ears on either side of your face and locate the TMJ by opening and closing your mouth slightly three or four times.

2 Keep feeling with your fingers, and now exaggerate the opening and closing of your mouth by doing it more slowly and widely. You should really be able to feel the TMJ now. Repeat three or four times.

1

3 Still holding the TMJ area with your fingers, move your jaw from side to side, slowly and carefully. This feels quite different and you may find that one side is more mobile because you tend to chew in that direction. Repeat three or four times.

4 Now, clench your teeth, hold for 3 seconds, then release. Feel with your fingers how that affects the TMJ area and the cheeks as well as the jaw. Repeat slowly three times.

5 Now, using your fingers, massage the TMJ area using slow and careful little circles. Keep your mouth relaxed and slightly open. Continue for about half a minute.

6 Take a few deep breaths, and relax, noting any sensations in your jaw or face. Notice how different the area feels after these exercises. Doing this routine regularly will help to prevent grinding of the teeth resulting from jaw tension.

breathe for your face

One of the most important gifts you can give your face is oxygen. If you sit inside all day in centrally heated or air-conditioned environments, your skin can get very dry, gray, and even slack because of lack of circulation. Here is a sequence of moves to get you breathing more deeply and improve your circulation. Do them outside if you can: it's a great way to start the day and be energized.

You know that going for a bracing walk makes your cheeks glow and your face tingle—these are signs of good oxygenation. If the skin circulation is good, cell renewal, and toxin removal are both greatly improved.

1 Stand with your feet shoulder-width apart and hold your arms parallel and straight out in front of you, palms facing downward. Stretch slightly into the position.

2 Breathing evenly and regularly, slowly move your arms up and down slightly several times. Keep your back and legs straight.

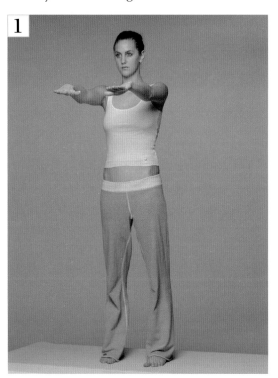

3 Now, increase the arc of the up and down movement slightly, so that your arms are moving from shoulder to waist height and back again. Don't go too fast—just find a pace you can manage comfortably. Repeat four times.

4 Now, extend even further, so that your arms travel from head to hip level. Keep breathing regularly and feel the muscles of your arms and torso warming up, your breathing deepening, and your circulation increasing. Repeat four times.

5 Stretch your arms and hands as high as you can above your head, still keeping your back straight.

6 Slowly curl forward and let your upper body relax down toward your toes, feeling the stretch in the back of your legs. Don't overstrain: go as far as you can, then slowly ease up.

After the exercise, stand in a relaxed pose and notice how you feel. You may experience sensations of warmth and a glowing feeling of vitality.

5

6

yoga postures to improve facial circulation

Some particular yoga postures (asanas) can really nourish and tone the face and neck. Here are two that you can try for a 10-minute yoga facelift. If you are new to yoga, please read the instructions carefully before you attempt the sequences, and note that correct breathing is important if you are to receive the maximum benefit.

shoulder stand (sarvangasana)

This asana encourages blood circulation from the feet to the face and head as well as stretching the neck. It should be avoided during menstruation. This posture is also not recommended if you have high blood pressure.

1 Lie down on the floor with your legs together, arms straight down, and palms flat on the floor by your sides. Breathe regularly and evenly.

2 Breathe in, then, on the exhalation, push down on the palms of your hands and lift your legs and hips off the floor, and over your head to an angle of about 45 degrees.

3 Straighten your legs out and support yourself with your hands under your lower back. Breathe evenly and stay in the posture for a few minutes, or for as long as you are comfortable.

4 To come out of the posture, relax your legs back to the angle of about 45 degrees, place your arms and hands back by your sides, and slowly roll down until you are lying flat again.

3

2

fish (matyasana)

This posture stretches the spine and works the sterno-cleido-mastoid muscles in the neck and chin, as well as encouraging circulation. If you are not very supple, slide a pillow under your lower back to help with this posture.

1 Lie flat on your back, legs together, and slide your arms under your back, with your hands flat under your buttocks. Breathe regularly and evenly.

2 Breathe in, then, as you exhale, push down on your hands and lift your upper back, arching so you can rest the top of your head on the floor. Breathe easily, staying in the posture for a few moments.

3 To release the posture, first uncurl your head and then lower your arms, so your back sinks down again to the floor. You will feel wonderfully straight, and also be aware of an increase in blood circulation around your face.

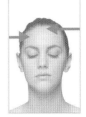

simple eastern
head massage

For facelift purposes, a head massage is a marvelous way to relax the whole head and face, improving circulation, and easing stress. This sequence is easy to give to yourself; you can do it on dry hair or try it in the shower with shampoo.

1 Place both hands in your hair on top of your head, and rest them there, breathing deeply. Feel the heat gather under your fingers—it's surprising how warm the top of the head is.

2 Move your hands in your hair slowly, making firm, circular massage movements all over the top, sides, and back of your skull.

Use your thumbs and fingertips to get good pressure, stimulating the scalp and muscles over the skull.

3 Using the heels of your hands, massage slowly and deeply in the area just above your ears, making circles one way and then the other. Your cheek muscles actually connect in here.

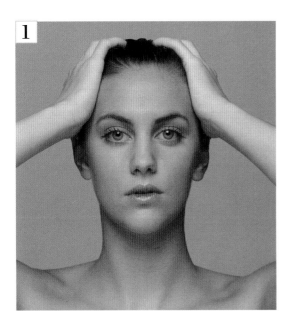

In India, China, and the Far East, head massage is a part of everyday life. People of all ages exchange it with each other. As well as stimulating the scalp, head massage works on muscles that attach to the skull; these can contribute to headaches or migraines if they remain tense. Eastern head massage is marvelous as a nourishing and nurturing self-treatment. Relieving stress also has an important part to play in facial rejuvenation.

4 Bring the heels of your hands to your temples and repeat the same circular movements—these areas respond well to

touch, and a lot of tension is stored here. You are improving muscle tone and circulation close to your eyes.

5 Use your thumbs to massage deeply at the base of the skull behind the ears; this action is wonderfully beneficial to the circulation of the neck and jaw area and helps to prevent migraine.

6 Finally, stroke your head from front to back, running your hands through your hair slowly. This feels very soothing and makes you feel that you are taking care of yourself.

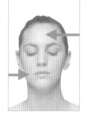

eastern energy holds
for facial vitality

Here are some simple ways to place your hands to re-energize your face. The hands do not massage or press, they simply hold the head or face in the described positions. This sequence is best performed lying down flat, somewhere comfortable, covered in a blanket so that you can really relax and keep warm. Use the routine to help yourself unwind.

1 Place both hands on the sides of your head, holding it gently, and relax for a few minutes. Your hands will feel very warm. This hold is a simple and instant way to unwind.

2 Place your fingertips gently in the middle of your forehead between the hairline and

your eyebrows, and hold for a few minutes. This hold is wonderful for relieving stress, easing mental chatter, and soothing headaches.

3 Place your fingertips directly between your eyebrows, and hold for a few moments. This hold will help relax and soothe

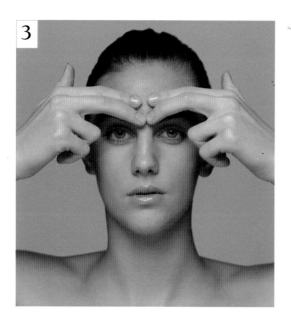

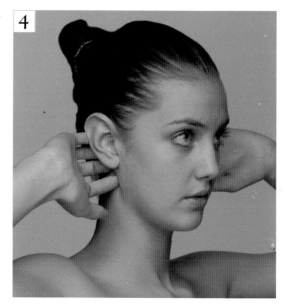

you if you have had to use a lot of mental concentration or if your eyes feel very tired.

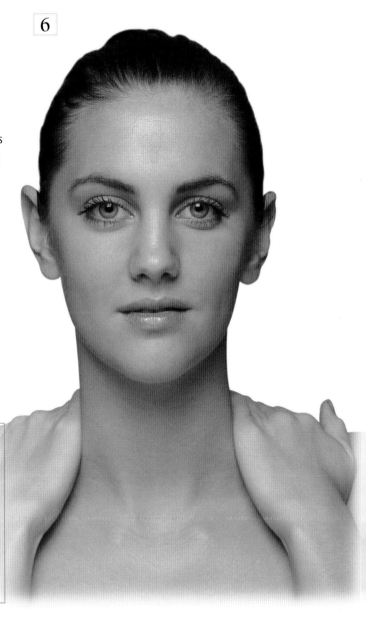

6

4 Place both hands behind your neck with your fingertips behind your ears, and hold for a few moments. You may feel a slight pulsing under your fingertips; wait until it calms to a steady rhythm. This hold is deeply relaxing and can help ease tension headaches.

5 Place your right hand on top of your head and your left hand cradling under your chin. This hold makes you very aware of the energy building in the face.

6 Rest both hands over the tops of your shoulders, imagining them relaxing down and loosening. Rest for a few more moments and enjoy the benefits of peace and calm.

energy for health

Traditional medicines in the Far East use the principle that we have a physical and an energetic body that work together. The physical body has areas—sometimes called points, or energy centers—where the energy of the nonphysical body can be used to rebalance the physical body. Acupuncturists place needles in specific locations to achieve this. Hands and fingers are also used to achieve this rebalancing using acupressure.

sleep simple nourishment for the face

Poor-quality sleep prevents our self-regenerating mechanisms from repairing and restoring us at cellular level and our circulation from carrying nutrients throughout the body, resulting in a tired and dull complexion. Sleeping difficulties can be helped by adopting a simple relaxing routine at the end of the day, designed to help you unwind.

Before performing this pre-sleep routine, have a relaxing warm bath or shower, and a warm drink such as a herbal tea made with chamomile or lime flower, or a simple mug of warm milk with a sprinkle of nutmeg on top. Get yourself comfortable in bed, with only a very dim light on, and no music or TV to distract you. Pause between each step and breathe easily for a moment before continuing.

1 Lie on your back with a low pillow under your head. Close your eyes and breathe regularly and evenly.

2 Start by tensing all the muscles in your legs and feet, hold this position for a few moments, then slowly release.

3 Tense your arms and clench your hands into fists, hold this position for a few minutes, then slowly release.

4 Tense the muscles in your abdomen for a few moments, then slowly release.

5 Tense your shoulders and hunch them up toward your ears, hold this position for a few moments, then slowly release.

6 Finally, screw your face up into a grimace, hold this position for a few moments, then slowly release.

When you have finished, lie still and simply breathe, noticing how your body feels… you may find that you fall asleep before the end, which is, of course, the ideal end to a presleep routine! Relaxed muscles will help you to obtain good-quality sleep and all the nourishment that brings.

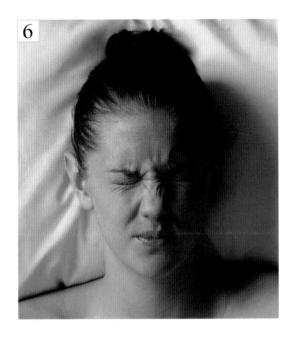

use light for
vitality and energy

In our modern society we find that we are spending much less time outside. This is because our work, travel, and living habits take us from one internal environment to another, all full of recycled air and artificial light. Our answer to this kind of existence is to jet off for a short period of time each year to locations where the sun is extremely powerful, and then proceed to expose all our skin to that intensity of sunlight. This practice is not good for the skin and encourages damage through burning, as well as cellular damage and premature aging, which is why using powerful sunscreens is important when on vacation.

However, full-spectrum light—daylight, especially when the sun is at its peak, around midday—is actually scientifically proven to be vital to overall health. People suffering from SAD (Seasonal Affective Disorder) are depressed and low because of light deprivation. Studies have shown that going out for a walk, even for just 10 minutes each lunchtime, exposes you to enough full-spectrum daylight to counter feelings of depression, low energy, or even premenstrual syndrome. Light acts on the pineal gland in your skull, which is linked to your pituitary gland that controls the balance of hormones in your body.

Moderate exposure to sunlight at the latitude where you normally live is actually beneficial to your skin; it encourages a healthy glow and helps to heal blemishes, as well as assisting the body to manufacture Vitamin D, which you need for bone formation. Obviously we expose our skin less in the colder months, and as the seasons warm up, we can slowly accustom our skin to the sun. Well–established health spas in Europe recommend spending regular time in strong light on a daily basis.

So give yourself a free 10-minute treat of light each day for health, vitality, and a radiant skin. It's easy to do, fits in with any schedule, and helps you to stay positive, even in the long winter months. It may be a very simple thing to do, but you will be making an important contribution to improving your health and well-being.

facial rejuvenation massage

This chapter will show you how to massage
your face and neck in a wide variety of ways,
incorporating different techniques and
ingredients to help your muscles and skin.
Face massage is vital for facial rejuvenation.
It works on the underlying tissues,
encouraging good blood supply, oxygenation,
delivery of nutrients, and removal of toxins,
and also reconditions and nourishes the
skin. Each of the individual routines takes
10 minutes to perform; you can select
massage ideas that interest you or choose
routines according to your skin type or facial
needs. The important thing to remember
is that you need to practice your routines
regularly to see a facelifting effect.

what you need for massage

In order to perform the massage routines in this chapter, you will need some lubricating ingredients to use on your skin. These are carrier oils, such as pure vegetable oils, which nourish the skin, and essential oils (pure natural plant fragrances), which are the basis of aromatherapy. Some routines use just carrier oils, while others use blends of both oils.

5 KEY CARRIER OILS

Apricot kernel: light and nourishing, excellent for mature or dry skins

Camellia: excellent silky oil for all skin types

Grape seed: nongreasy, useful for well-lubricated skin

Jojoba: golden liquid wax, suitable for all skin types

Sweet almond: helps dry and undernourished skins (not advised for people with nut allergies)

a brief word on safety

Essential oils are used in very weak dilutions on the face, so that blends are safe even if you are pregnant. Do not expose your skin to sunlight for 12 hours after applying any blends containing citrus oils. Essential oils should be kept in a cool dark place, well out of reach of children. After opening, essential oils will last up to 6 months at room temperature and 1 year in the refrigerator.

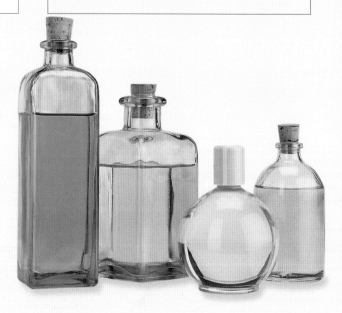

14 KEY ESSENTIAL OILS

Fennel (*Foeniculum vulgare*): deep-cleanses and detoxifies all skin types

Frankincense (*Boswellia carterii*): tones and rejuvenates all skin types

Geranium (*Pelargonium graveolens*): balances and hydrates oily and combination skins

Grapefruit (*Citrus x paradisi*): tones and detoxifies all skin types

Juniper berry (*Juniperus communis*): detoxifies and deep-cleanses all skin types

Lavender (*Lavandula angustifolia*): tones combination, oily, and blemish-prone skins

Lemon (*Citrus limon*): tones and tightens pores in oily and combination skins

Mandarin (*Citrus reticulata*): tones and clarifies oily and combination skins

Orange blossom (*Citrus x aurantium*): hydrates and nourishes dry, mature, and sensitive skins

Palmarosa (*Cymbopogon martinii*): soothes sensitive, allergy-prone skins

Rose (*Rosa damascena*): cools and soothes all skin types

Rosewood (*Aniba roseaodora*): soothes and nourishes dry and mature skins

Sandalwood (*Santalum album*): cools and hydrates dry and mature skins

Tea tree (*Melaleuca alternifolia*): cleanses and disinfects all skin types

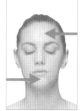

basic face massage
part 1

If you have never tried massage before, it is useful to learn some simple strokes before you begin. Massage is a special form of touch that works specifically to increase blood flow to muscles, easing away toxins, and releasing tension. In face work, you need to get used to working on small muscles with precise movements.

This simple massage uses the first and most basic massage movement—stroking. It involves the fingertips and palms of the hands. To massage comfortably, it is best to have short nails.

For the massage, use 1 teaspoon (5 ml) of carrier oil, such as apricot kernel, to lubricate the skin.

1 **Stroking up from the chin** Start with your hands on either side of the face; with your palms and fingertips, stroke slowly up the sides of the face and up to the forehead, then glide back down again lightly. Repeat three times. The emphasis in the movement is pressure up the face, and then easing off.

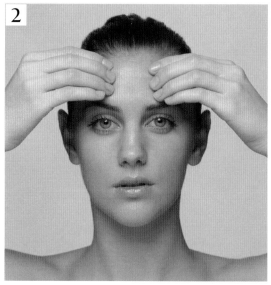

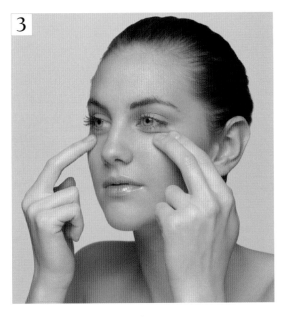

2 Stroking out over the forehead Place your fingertips together in the middle of your forehead, then press firmly and glide out to the sides; lift the fingers off, return to the starting pose, and repeat three times. This movement smoothes out the forehead.

3 Stroking around the eyes Using only a minimal amount of oil to ease the movement, place your fingertips at the sides of your eyes and stroke around the bony edge of the eye socket. Work up over the eyebrows, down the center of the nose, under the eyes, and back to the starting position. Repeat three times. This movement helps to improve eyestrain, and the oil will lubricate the skin around the eye area.

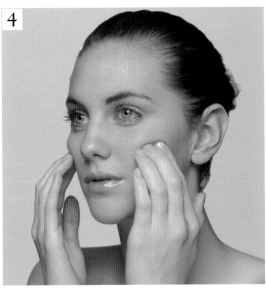

4 Stroking under the cheekbones Starting close to the nose, with your hands on the inner side of each cheek, make small circular pressures all the way out toward your ears. Give special attention to the area just under the ear (the location of the temporo-mandibular joint), then massage back toward the nose. Repeat the sequence three times. This movement tones the cheek muscles, which work hard every day.

basic face massage
part 2

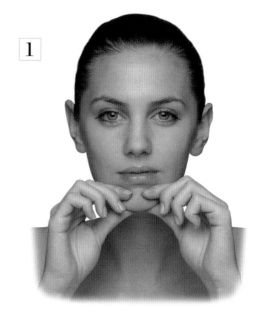

This massage can be used immediately after the stroking on pages 48–49 to create a full-face massage. It involves movements that work more deeply than the previous ones, but it is safe to do so because the skin has already been warmed by the stroking exercises. These techniques are very toning to the complexion and start the facial rejuvenation process.

For the massage, add a little more apricot kernel carrier oil to your fingers—no more than 1 teaspoon (5 ml) should be needed. The aim is to have enough oil on your hands to work smoothly, without leaving the skin feeling slippery. Note, too, that you could use your favorite night cream instead for these two basic massage routines. In this way, you apply your cream, not only feeding all the beneficial ingredients deep into your skin, but your skin and muscles also get the benefits of the massage.

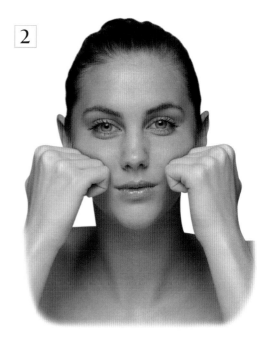

1 **Kneading the chin** Starting with your hands in the middle of your chin, with your fingertips facing outward and your thumbs

under your chin, make small kneading movements all the way along your jaw, out toward your ears, and back to the middle. Repeat three times. This movement tones the muscles and circulation of the jaw area.

2 **Knuckling the cheeks** Make your hands into loose fists and knuckle the area just under your cheekbones for a few minutes, using slow and deliberate movements, first in one direction then the other. You will be able to feel your teeth under the muscles of the cheeks; notice any tension in this area as you work. Many people grind their teeth at night, so these muscles may ache with this movement.

3 **Circling the forehead** Using the heels of your hands, make large, deliberate circles over your forehead, first one way then the other. Keep this movement slow and give it firm pressure. This movement really works the forehead area, and can also ease tension headaches, which cause frowning.

4 **Tapping the face** End the routine by using your fingertips to tap lightly all over your face from the forehead down over the cheeks to the chin. This movement is very soothing and stimulates all the energy zones in your face, making you feel awake and refreshed mentally, with tingling skin.

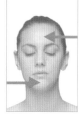

deep circulation
stimulating routine

This routine is especially good for mature skins that look dull or pale due to poor circulation. A good blood supply is vital for supplying nutrients to the skin, particularly the inner layer (dermis), where a vast network of tiny blood vessels floods the skin with fresh circulation. This routine gives a glow to the complexion.

Before performing this routine, try a simple oatmeal scrub to gently exfoliate the skin surface. In a small bowl, place 2 tablespoons (30 ml) of fine oatmeal, and add enough water to mix to a paste. Apply this mixture to your face with small circular movements, avoiding the eye area, and then remove with warm water and pat your skin dry.

For the blend, use 1 teaspoon (5 ml) of nourishing jojoba carrier oil with 1 drop of frankincense essential oil for cell renewal.

1 **Pressing across the forehead** Bring your index fingers together to meet in the middle of your forehead at your hairline. Make a line of pressures out toward the sides of the forehead. Then bring the fingertips back together, a little farther down, and make a second line of pressures out to the sides of the forehead. Continue until you reach eyebrow level. (Four lines of horizontal pressures are usually enough.)

2 **Pressing down the sides of the nose** Bring the tips of your index fingers together between your eyebrows and stroke slowly down the sides of your nose, pressing firmly, to the

level of your mouth. Lift your fingers off and repeat the movement three times. Sometimes this area can be a little tender, so be gentle.

3 **Stretching and lifting the cheeks** Using all your fingertips, with one hand on either side of your nose, stroke out over the cheeks to the sides of your face, stretching the skin under your hands, then release. Repeat this movement three times.

4 **Alternate stroking under the chin** Using one hand after the other, slowly and firmly stroke up the neck and under the chin in a series of sweeping movements. Keep the strokes firm and flowing. This stroke encourages good muscle tone in the chin and lower jaw area and is vital for lifting sagging skin.

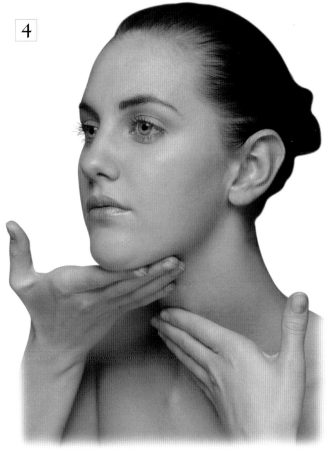

detoxification routine

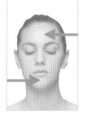

This routine improves overoily or blemish-prone skin with a combination of skin-cleansing ingredients and massage movements to encourage the drainage of toxins. It uses sweeping movements down the face to enhance detoxification via the lymphatic glands in the sides of the neck.

Before the massage, try a special facial steam to deep-cleanse the face. Pour 4 cups of near-boiling water into a heatproof glass bowl, and add 2 tablespoons (30 ml) of dried chamomile flowers. Remove contact lenses, if wearing. Lean over the bowl with your head under a towel, and let the soothing steam bathe your face for 10 minutes. Rinse your face afterward with warm water and pat dry.

For the blend, combine 1 teaspoon (5 ml) of jojoba carrier with 1 drop of cleansing lemon essential oil.

1 Wide circles down the face First, to apply the lemon-scented oil, make wide circular movements across your forehead, down your cheeks and nose to your chin. These strokes need to spread the oil over the whole surface of the face. Work from the middle of the face outward to encourage drainage.

1

2 Small circles from the cheeks down Working from under the eyes down to the chin, make a series of lines of small circular pressures, working outward in horizontal lines from the nose area to the sides of the face. You will probably find that four horizontal lines of pressures will be enough to travel from under your eyes to your chin.

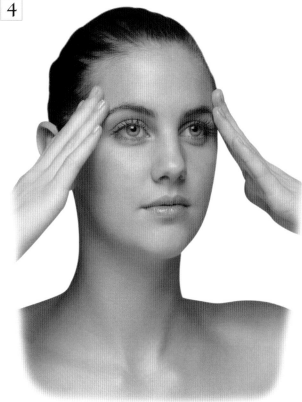

3 **Alternate cheek movement** With a hand on each cheek, make a series of large circles on alternate cheeks, moving the whole cheek area each time. Keep this stroke slow but the pressure firm. This movement exercises the muscles in the cheeks, chin, and jaw. Repeat several times, and feel how your whole face loosens up.

4 **Sweeping strokes down the face** Starting at your forehead, with fingertips meeting in the middle, stroke slowly all the way down the sides of your face to the chin and then sweep down to the neck. Bring the fingers back to the starting point and repeat the whole movement three more times. This movement encourages the drainage of toxins from the face.

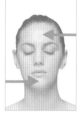

deep facial
rejuvenation routine

This routine is a lovely facial treat that is particularly suited to dry and mature skin types. It can be given once or twice a week to nourish and revive the complexion and tone the facial structure. If you work in a very dehydrating environment, then this treatment will help to ease the effects of heating or air-conditioning.

Before the massage, thoroughly cleanse and tone your skin. Soak a clean face cloth in hand-hot water combined with 2 drops of soothing lavender essential oil; wring out any excess water and place the hot face cloth over your face for a minute to gently hydrate and open your pores.

For the blend, prepare 2 teaspoons (10 ml) of sweet almond oil with 1 drop of frankincense and 1 drop of mandarin essential oil stirred in to tone and revitalize your face.

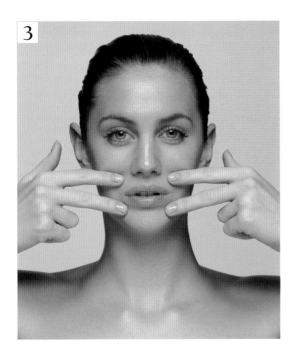

1 **Cupping the face** With a little oil blend on your hands, cup one hand over your forehead and one under your chin. Hold for a few moments, relax, breathe deeply, and inhale the aroma of the blend. Gradually smooth the blend over the upper and lower halves of the face using your fingertips.

2 **Alternate stroking up the cheeks** Starting at chin level, make sweeping upward strokes on one cheek using both hands alternately, one following the other, then transfer across to the other side. This movement helps to improve circulation as well as toning the muscles of the cheek and chin area, increasing lift. It is also a very relaxing and soothing stroke.

3 **Stretching around the mouth** Use your index and middle fingers in a V shape placed around your mouth. Slowly draw the fingers apart and out over your cheeks; release, come back to the starting position, and repeat three times. This movement helps to massage the ring of muscle around the mouth and ease out fine lines.

4 **Alternate upward strokes on the forehead** Using the palms of your hands one after the other, stroke firmly and slowly up the forehead using alternate movements, one hand following the other. As well as smoothing out lines, this move is also very soothing for headaches or eyestrain. Repeat the movements for 2 minutes.

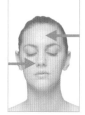

acupressure routine
for facial toning

Acupressure concentrates movements on energy lines called meridians. These are channels of chi, or life-force energy, which circulates through the physical body every 24 hours. Points on the meridians can become blocked due to physical and emotional pressure, and acupressure helps to relieve the obstruction and move the energy through the channels once more.

Use just the pads of the fingers or thumbs for this treatment. Pressure is firm and there is no massage, just simple "on" and "off" movements. Hold each point for 3 seconds, then release. There is no need for carrier oils or other ingredients, but the techniques are best worked on clean skin.

1 **Points down the middle of the forehead**
Starting at the middle of the forehead at the hairline, use your middle finger to apply firm pressure for 3 seconds, then release; repeat twice. Move down to the middle of the forehead, apply pressure, and repeat twice. Then move down to the middle point between the eyebrows, apply pressure, and repeat twice. These points all help to discourage frowning and ease headaches.

2 Points on either side of the nose Place your index fingers next to the base of your nose by the nostrils. Press firmly for 3 seconds, then release. Repeat twice. These points can be sore, as a great deal of facial tension is stored here; working here can also ease toothache and sinus trouble.

3 Point in the middle of the upper lip Place one index finger in the groove above the upper lip and apply pressure, then release.

Repeat twice. This point tones the lip area as well as helping to prevent weight gain by regulating hunger cravings.

4 Points at the temples Use three fingers together, with one hand on each of your temples. Press inward firmly and gently, then release. Repeat twice. These points increase energy and blood flow to the eye area and also improve alertness and concentration.

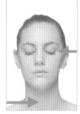

acupressure routine
for inner beauty

Pressure point techniques from the Far East can regulate the oils and moisture in the skin as well as assisting with hormonal balance in the body. These points are deceptively simple, and yet they are vital to facial rejuvenation because they work inside as well as outside the face. This routine provides an energizing and harmonizing start to your day.

As previously, you do not need a carrier oil for this routine—simply apply the pressure for 3 seconds, then release. Use the pads of your fingers and thumbs to apply the pressure.

1 **Finger pressures inside the eye sockets** Place your index fingers on the sides of your nose just near the inner edge of the eyes. Press gently for 3 seconds, then release. Repeat twice. This move is deeply relaxing to the area and can help to ease eyestrain caused by too much close work.

2 **Finger pressures on the TMJ and edge of the eye sockets** Place your thumbs on your TMJ (temporo-mandibular joint) area and your

index fingers on the outside bony edge of your eye sockets. Open your mouth slightly and press into the points for 3 seconds, then release. Repeat twice. These points help to release tension in the jaw and eye areas on the sides of the face.

3 **Finger pressures in the center of the cheeks** Using all your fingertips together, press upward and inward under both

1

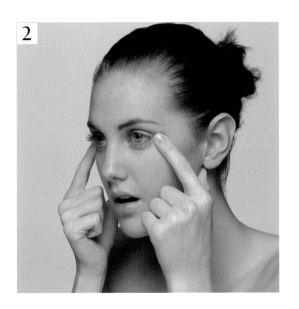

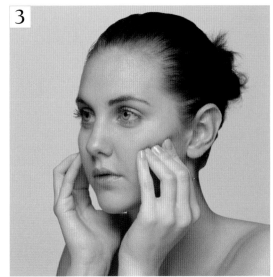

cheekbones. You will be able to feel your teeth under the layers of muscle tissue. Hold for 3 seconds, release, then repeat twice. These points help to regulate the digestive function and can also help to control appetite and cravings.

4 **Fingers over the thyroid area** Women in the Far East have traditionally held these points every day to maintain their beauty. With your right hand, place your fingers and thumb over the dip in your clavicle. Press very gently inward—not too hard—for 3 seconds, then release; repeat twice. The points here help to balance hormones in the body.

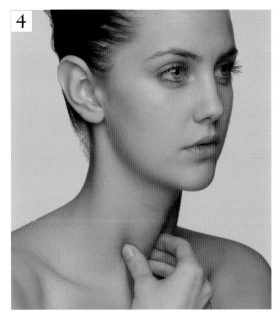

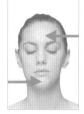

eastern-style nourishing
face routine

This routine is based on moves from Ayurvedic massage, which is thousands of years old and still practiced today in India. Ayurveda is a combination of energetic and physical techniques designed to promote optimum health. This massage will deeply relax the face, and will increase the flow of blood and prana, or life-force energy, to the facial area.

For the blend, place 2 teaspoons (10 ml) of carrier oil in a small dish and add 2 drops of either pure rose or sandalwood essential oil. Sweet almond oil is recommended because it is nourishing and does not leave a sticky residue, unlike some carriers used in Ayurvedic massage.

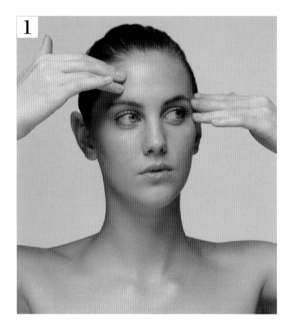

1 **Alternate rubbing across the face** Using your index and middle fingers together, and starting at the forehead, make a series of alternate strokes horizontally across the area, moving slowly down the right side of your face, across the chin and mouth area, up the left side, and back to the forehead. Repeat the circuit. These movements will energize the whole face.

2 **Alternate finger stroking down the nose** Starting between your eyebrows and using your index fingers, make very tiny alternate strokes down the bridge of your nose, then on the right and left sides for a few moments. These strokes work the blend into an area prone to wrinkles.

3 **Finger pulsing movement** Place the fingertips of both hands at the top of your forehead, touching the skin, then move them slightly up and down to create a pulsing effect. Do not move your fingers across the skin: keep them in the same place, but move the skin

beneath them over your skull. Now gradually move down the forehead to the cheeks and chin with the pulsing movement, lifting the fingers off, and replacing them a little farther down each time until you have covered the whole face, then repeat. This sequence really helps to tone the facial muscles.

4 **Face cupping** To finish, cup your left hand over your forehead and your right hand under your chin. Breathe deeply for a few moments, feeling the flow of energy in your face, and inhaling the aroma of the blend.

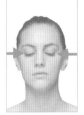

eastern-style massage
to the eye area

The eye area is one of the first places to show signs of aging, such as wrinkles, sagging skin, and dark circles. Indian traditional massage not only treats this area with fine nutrients and natural ingredients but also helps to stimulate vital energy supplies to other parts of the body via energy channels similar to meridians.

For the blend, place 2 teaspoons (10 ml) of apricot kernel oil in a small dish, and stir in 2 drops of either orange blossom or geranium essential oil for additional harmonizing and skin-soothing effects. It is important when you do this massage that no blend gets into the eye, as this could cause irritation.

1 Finger strokes around the eye areas
Coat your fingertips with the blend and gently stroke it all around the bony eye sockets, starting at the inside end of the eyebrows and working out to the sides, under the eyes, up the inside of the nose, and back again. Repeat this movement several times to nourish and soothe these areas.

2 Circular pressures on the outer eye areas
Place your middle fingers carefully next to the outer corner of each eye. Apply slow and gentle circular pressure in a clockwise direction, taking care not to get the blend into the eye. This eases eyestrain and improves muscle tone.

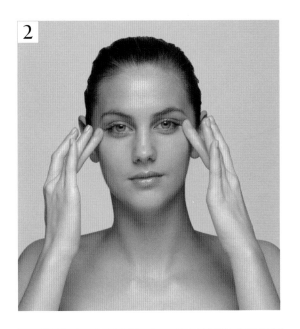

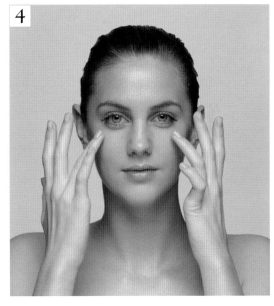

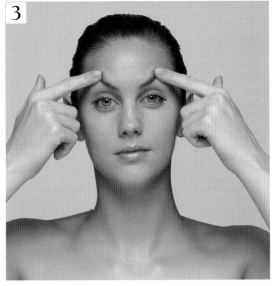

3 **Circular pressures in the middle of the eyebrows** Place one index finger in the middle of each eyebrow. Apply firm circular pressures in one direction, then reverse. Pressure on this area improves not only muscle tone and blood supply to the eyes but also mental clarity and function.

4 **Patting the eye areas** Using the fingertips, gently pat all around both eye areas, with a touch as light as drops of water. Continue patting for a few moments, going around the eyes about three times. This action gently stimulates circulation and energizes the area.

special neck-toning
routine

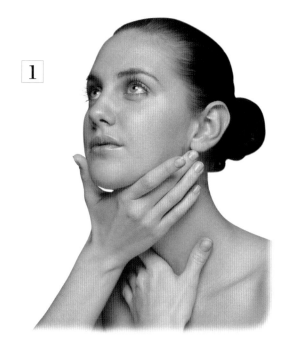

This routine is devoted to toning and supporting the muscles and skin in the neck area, particularly for more mature complexions. Neck massage is easy to do for yourself and eases away all the tension of a long day, as well as toning and firming areas prone to sagging. This sequence works well at nighttime after a bath or shower.

For the blend, place 2 teaspoons (10 ml) of jojoba carrier oil in a small dish and add 2 drops of frankincense essential oil for extra muscle toning and uplifting effects. Jojoba is a nourishing carrier for all skin types, even those that are naturally well lubricated.

1 **Sweeping strokes up the front of the neck** Using the palms of both hands, stroke all the way up the neck from the clavicle to the chin, one hand following the other in a series of slow and precise movements. Try to apply gentle pressure as you move up the neck to really tone and lift the muscles.

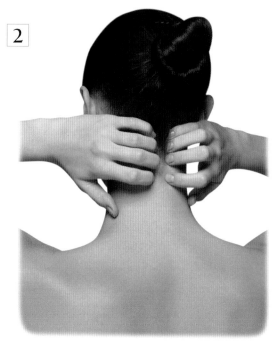

2 **Fingertip circles around the bones in the neck** Place your fingertips just under your skull so that they rest on either side of the spinal bones (vertebrae) in the neck. Gently make tiny circular movements and travel down the length of the neck, really working into any areas that feel tense. This sequence helps to maintain the correct posture of the neck.

3 **Sweeping movements up the sides of the neck** Using one hand on each side, and starting at the outside edge of the shoulder, sweep up the sides of the neck and down again several times, keeping a slow, rhythmical movement. This movement helps to ease out the sterno-cleido-mastoid muscle between the shoulder and chin area.

4 **Lift and stretch the neck** Place both hands behind your neck, resting under your skull. Slowly lift upward so there is a gentle stretch to your neck, hold for 3 seconds, then release. Repeat the movement three times. Again, this stretch improves posture, which is essential for the neck.

3

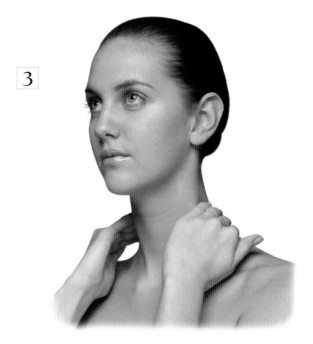

4

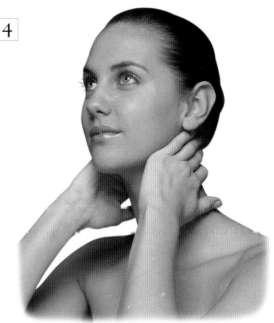

hydrotherapy routine
to deep-cleanse

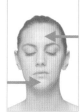

Sometimes normal cleansing is not enough and you want to deep-cleanse your face, especially if your skin is oily, you have blocked pores, or are prone to blemishes. Hydrotherapy uses water in combination with other ingredients, heated to different temperatures, to achieve cleansing, toning, and stimulating effects on the skin and underlying muscles.

For the blend, place a small glass bottle containing 2 teaspoons (10 ml) of apricot kernel carrier oil with 2 drops of toning mandarin essential oil in a small bowl of hot water. Leave the bottle in the hot water so that the blend will be warm when it goes on your skin.

1 **Steaming the face** Pour 2½ cups of near-boiling water into a heatproof glass bowl and add 3 drops of cleansing lavender essential oil. Remove contact lenses, if wearing. Lean over the bowl with your head under a towel and allow the fragrant steam to bathe your face and open the pores. Remain for 3 minutes, lifting the towel for fresh air.

2 **Cold water splash** Now, splash cold water all over your face—it will feel very tingling and invigorating, and the contrast in temperature will contract the blood vessels, toning your whole face. Pat your skin dry, noticing how it feels.

3 **Fingertip circles with the blend** Take your warm carrier oil and apply it all over your face with small circular massage movements, really working it into any areas where the skin needs attention or where there are wrinkles. Feel how the skin absorbs the blend and notice the sensation of the carrier oil as you apply it.

4 **Finger drainage movements** Place your index fingers flat together in the middle of your forehead, and slowly push outward to the sides of the face. Repeat over the cheeks and finally the chin. These movements encourage toxins to come out of the tissues.

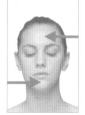

deep facial
cooling routine

This routine incorporates a mask made with blended cucumber, which is amazingly soothing and hydrating to the skin, as well as cooling. This is followed by the application of a layer of aloe vera gel enriched with nourishing essential oils. Aloe gel is astonishingly soothing, has well-known skin healing properties, and is easily obtained from good health food stores. This cooling routine is very helpful for sensitive, allergy-prone skins because it uses very simple ingredients and is nourishing to delicate complexions.

For the blend, place 1 tablespoon (15 ml) of aloe vera gel in a dish and stir in 1 drop of palmarosa and 1 drop of orange blossom essential oil. This mixture will be used after the mask.

For the mask, take half a cucumber, wash it thoroughly, and cut off two slices. Chop the rest into small pieces and blend thoroughly. The mask is now ready to use.

1 **Cooling and hydrating mask** Spread some of the blended cucumber paste over your face and place the two slices of cucumber over your eyes. Lie down for 5 minutes to allow the cooling effects to be felt. Then remove the slices, rinse off the mask with lukewarm water, and gently pat the skin dry.

1

2 **Application of aloe gel** Gently smooth the lightly scented aloe vera gel over your face in a thin layer. Because the gel is so full of water, it can be left on the skin to be absorbed for a few moments—you will be surprised at how quickly it disappears. Notice how soothing it feels.

3 **Gentle fingertip massage** Using only the fingertips, use the pulsing movements from the Eastern-style massage on pages 64–65 to work slowly down the whole face. Remember, this massage improves the flow of energy to the whole area and helps the absorption of the essential oils.

4 **Sweeping strokes down to the chin** End the routine with a few sweeping strokes from the forehead down to the chin, which will gently soothe and calm the skin. Rest for a few moments to feel the effects of the mask and the gel, and notice how your skin feels now. The texture should be very soft, and the surface should feel cool and moist.

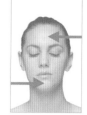

special aromatherapy
routine for dry skin

Aromatherapy takes facial rejuvenation massage a whole step further. So far we have used extremely simple blends of carrier oil with a tiny amount of essential oil added to them. Now we shall use blends of essential oils that are directly linked to skin types. The first one is dry skin, which, as we have seen, tends to be very taut and is susceptible to reddening in wind or sun.

For the blend, place 2 teaspoons (10 ml) of apricot kernel oil in a dish, add 1 drop of rose, and 1 drop of sandalwood essential oil and stir together. These essential oils soothe and hydrate the upper skin layers, repairing, and protecting vulnerable dry skin. If your skin is extremely dry, try piercing one evening primrose oil capsule and squeezing the contents into your blend as well for extra nourishment.

1 **Cleanse and tone the skin** You can use your normal cleanser and toner to prepare the skin for the massage, or you can use

1 teaspoon (5 ml) of jojoba with 1 drop of mandarin essential oil. Apply this mixture with a cotton wool pad to cleanse away impurities. Follow with a cotton wool pad soaked in orange flower water.

2 **Applying the blend** Use circling movements with the tips of your fingers to spread the blend all over the face, taking care to work it in well over very dry areas. Feel the texture of the oil, how it penetrates the skin and leaves it feeling silky, and inhale the gentle aroma of the essential oils.

3 **Knuckling the face** To work a little deeper, use slow knuckling movements, especially over the cheeks and chin. This movement really works the essential oils more deeply into the skin, down to the muscle layer beneath. Make sure you work well over any areas affected by dryness.

4 **Palming the face** Hold the hands gently over the face, not applying any pressure. This action is very soothing, and the warmth that builds up under the hands helps the absorption of the blend and the essential oils by opening the pores. You can also lie down for a few minutes and palm the face in that position, which is emotionally very relaxing.

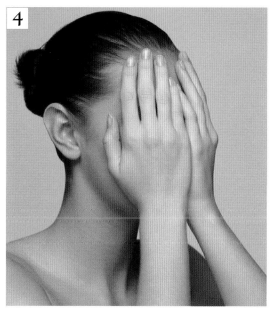

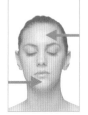

special aromatherapy
routine for mature skin

This routine is designed to have a renewing and toning effect on skin and muscles that may be showing signs of tiredness or slackness, or lines and wrinkles. This blend needs to be applied daily for at least a month for you to see real improvements, and it is best used at nighttime to allow maximum absorption of the ingredients. Frankincense has been used since ancient Egyptian times as an aromatic ingredient to repair and beautify the complexion—it is said that Cleopatra had a personal supply from her own gardens.

For the blend, place 2 teaspoons (10 ml) of camellia oil (a very fine vegetable oil from the Far East, used for centuries to condition skin and hair) in a dish and stir in 1 drop of frankincense and 1 drop of orange blossom essential oil. This combination encourages cell renewal, improves and tones local circulation, and helps the face to glow.

1 **Cleanse and tone the skin** You can prepare your skin for the treatment using your regular cleanser and toner, or you can use 1 teaspoon (5 ml) of jojoba with 1 drop of sandalwood essential oil in it on a cotton wool pad to cleanse, followed by an application of pure rosewater to tone and hydrate.

2 **Apply the blend** Use alternate strokes up the face, one hand following the other, first on the right side then on the left side,

to encourage healthy circulation and improve muscle tone. Spread the blend carefully into any areas where the face is slack or lined, or where the skin is dull in texture.

3 **Deep finger pressures** Starting at the chin, slowly apply deep circular pressures up the sides of the face toward the forehead, working with one hand on each side of the face. Repeat the sequence. Here you are working more into the lower layers, encouraging good blood supply and toxin removal.

4 **Sweeping strokes down the face** Starting at the forehead, sweep the hands downward to the chin and neck, encouraging waste products to drain away from the face after the massage.

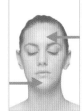

special aromatherapy
routine for oily skin

Essential oils are fabulous to use on oily skin because they can regulate the production of the skin's own lubrication, called sebum, which can so often lead to clogged pores or even blemishes. Also, it is possible to make lovely smelling blends for oily skin that are pleasant to use and very effective. This blend is fresh and soft smelling and has a positive effect on the mind as well as the skin. The carrier used here is jojoba, which is a liquid wax, not a vegetable oil, and does not leave a shiny residue.

For the blend, place 2 teaspoons (10 ml) of jojoba carrier in a dish and stir in 1 drop of lemon and 1 drop of geranium essential oil; this combination is cleansing and also balances oil production. Note that, because this blend contains lemon essential oil, which can cause skin reactions in strong sunlight, it should be applied at night. If it is used during the day, you should avoid direct sunlight for 12 hours.

1 **Steam treatment** Place 2½ cups of near-boiling water in a heatproof bowl and add 2 drops of juniper berry and 2 drops of grapefruit essential oil to deep-cleanse. Remove contact lenses, if wearing. Lean over the bowl with your head under a towel for 5 minutes, then rinse the skin and pat dry. This treatment should leave the complexion tingling.

1

2 Apply the blend Use the fingertips to work the blend all over the face; small circular movements are best. Ensure you apply it thoroughly and feel how the jojoba is absorbed, leaving a soft and silky finish. The essential oils also begin to work their way into the deeper layers.

3 Smoothing the skin With one hand on each side of the face, use the fingers to smooth the skin out toward the sides of the face in one long deliberate stroke. This action encourages the drainage of toxins and tones the facial muscles. Repeat three times.

4 Tapping the face Use your fingertips to tap lightly all over your face, so that your skin feels invigorated and refreshed. Tap over all areas, including the forehead. This action can also be very stress relieving if your eyes are tired.

Your skin will feel very supple and fragrant after this treatment. If you do it two to three times a week, your pores will tighten and your skin will be well toned.

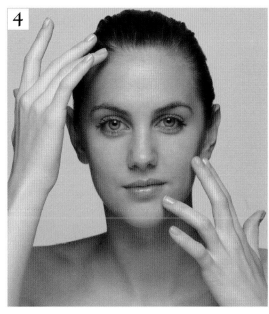

special aromatherapy
routine for combination skin

Combination skin can be helped significantly with the right essential oils. It is important for the blend to have a balancing effect on skin oil production, as well as a soothing and hydrating effect on drier areas. Essential oils in the right combination can achieve this. Often there is a hormonal link to changes in skin oiliness, and using aromatherapy regularly can help to restore your internal balance. There are two parts to this routine.

For the mask, wash and peel a ripe peach, chop it up, and blend with 3–4 tablespoons (45–60 ml) of good-quality honey to make a paste.

1

The fruit has a slightly astringent effect and the honey is moisturizing.

For the massage blend, add 1 drop of geranium and 1 drop of sandalwood essential oil to 2 tablespoons (30 ml) of sweet almond oil for a balancing and hydrating combination.

1 **Apply the mask** Smooth the peach and honey mask onto freshly cleansed skin: it will feel cooling and soothing. Leave it on for 5 minutes to get the maximum effect from the ingredients, then wash it off with warm water and pat the skin dry. It should already feel very soft and smooth.

2 **Apply the blend** Using circular fingertip strokes, work the blend all over the face, across all zones, especially into any particularly dry or oily areas. Keep working for a few moments, feeling the blend being absorbed into the skin, and inhaling the delicate aroma.

3 Work the nose and eye socket areas
Using just your index fingers, and starting at the inside of the eyebrows, stroke out to the edge of the bony eye socket areas, round under the eyes, and back up the sides of the nose. Repeat this stroke twice. This move gets the blend into typically oily areas.

4 Alternate circles over the cheeks
Using the palms of both hands, one on either side, make large circular movements over the whole cheek area, one side after the other, to massage the cheek muscles and work the blend into drier areas.

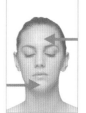

special aromatherapy
routine for normal skin

If you are lucky enough to have normal skin that is blemish free, peachy soft, and fine-textured, it is still important that you look after it. Use the nourishing and cell-renewing properties of essential oils to support and renew your complexion, and know that your skin is benefiting from really fine natural ingredients, free of any harsh chemicals. By using this routine regularly you will be maintaining and enhancing the quality of your skin, as well as working the facial muscles. This routine uses another nourishing mask, followed by a lovely aromatic and skin-soothing blend with essential oils.

For the mask, place 3 tablespoons (45 ml) of fine oatmeal in a small dish and mix with 2 tablespoons (30 ml) of plain yogurt. The slightly acidic nature of the yogurt will help to soften the skin's outer surface, while the oatmeal is soothing.

For the blend, place 2 teaspoons (10 ml) of camellia oil in a dish and add 1 drop of rose and 1 drop of mandarin essential oil for a softening and slightly toning effect.

1 **Apply the mask** After cleansing and toning your skin, carefully spread the mask all over the face, avoiding the inner eye area. Lie down and rest for 5 minutes to allow the ingredients to soak into the skin, then rinse the mask off with lukewarm water and pat the skin dry.

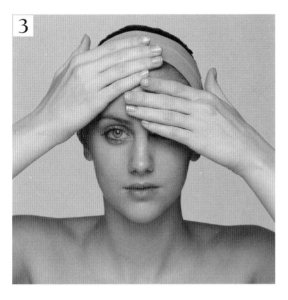

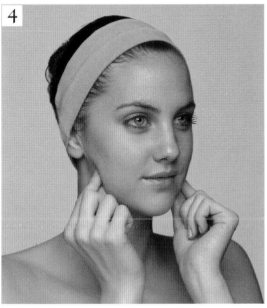

Apply the blend Smooth the blend all over your face, from the forehead down the cheeks, and down to the chin. Make sure you work it around the eye area but not too close to the eyes, to avoid irritation.

Alternate sweeping strokes upward Make long, sweeping strokes from chin level up the face, one hand following the other, first up the right side then the left, and also up the forehead. These strokes stimulate the circulation and improve muscle tone.

Kneading the chin area Using your index fingers and thumbs, knead slowly around the chin from the middle out to just under the ears and back again; repeat twice. This movement tones the muscles in the chin area and helps to prevent sagging.

This routine is a lovely nourishing treat. Try it two to three times a week for a peachy-soft and supple complexion with a soft glow.

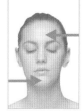

special aromatherapy
for blemish-prone skin

If your skin is prone to blemishes, cleanliness is vital on the outside surface, and good detoxification is important within. Try to drink several glasses of pure spring water every day to encourage good elimination and eat lots of fresh fruit and vegetables. This routine uses steaming, followed by an application of revitalizing and healing essential oils stirred into aloe vera gel for its cooling, soothing, and skin-healing properties. You will find the aloe gel is gently nourishing.

For the blend, place 2 teaspoons (10 ml) of aloe vera gel in a dish, and stir in 1 drop of grapefruit and 1 drop of frankincense essential oil for their antiseptic and skin-healing effects. You will notice that the essential oils combine very easily with the gel to create a softly aromatic preparation. The gel will help to heal and soothe the blemished areas of your face.

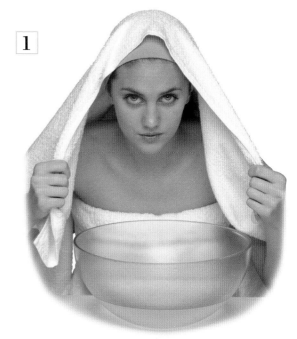

1 **Steaming for deep cleansing** Pour 2½ cups of near-boiling water into a heatproof bowl and add 2 drops of tea tree

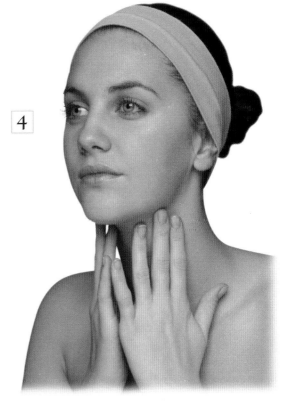

and 2 drops of lavender essential oil for their cleansing effects. Remove contact lenses, if wearing. Lean over the bowl with your head under a towel and the fragrant steam will heat the skin, opening the pores and removing toxins. Steam for 5 minutes, rinse the face with warm water, and pat the skin dry.

2 **Apply the aloe gel** Smooth the aromatic gel all over your face, being careful to avoid the inner eye area. Apply the gel as a layer and allow it to soak into the skin for a few moments. Feel how the skin tingles as the essential oils start to work.

3 **Pulsing over the face** Starting at the forehead, press lightly up and down with your fingertips, then move the fingers lower and repeat. Work your way down the face over the cheeks to the chin in this way. This movement will increase the blood supply to your face.

4 **Smoothing down the face** Stroke down the face from the forehead to the chin and neck several times to encourage the elimination of toxins from this area. Your skin should feel clean, soft, and energized, and any blemished areas soothed.

diet and the complexion

What you eat is vitally important to the appearance and structure of your face as well as to your general health and well-being. Enhancing beauty is not just a matter of taking care of the outside of the body—it is also about becoming more aware of what you put into your body and how it does or does not serve you. In this chapter, we look in detail at major skin stressors and examine how dietary measures can make a real difference to your features. You will find lots of mouth-watering ideas for skin treats that taste wonderful as well as providing skin-enhancing vitamins and minerals.

4

major skin stressors

Before we look more closely at dietary skin support, we need to familiarize ourselves with two very significant skin stressors. These are substances that we deliberately introduce into the body but that have a direct effect on skin cells, muscle tone, and consequently the whole appearance of the face. These stressors have a major impact because they are a part of lifestyle habits that can be challenging to change.

smoking

Cigarettes are the biggest culprit. There is a substance in them called benzopyrene that seriously depletes the body's store of vitamin C, which is vital to the formation of collagen—the fibers that make up the skin's support structure. So, quite simply, if you smoke regularly, your skin will start to wrinkle. Research suggests that smokers' skin ages up to 20 years sooner than that of nonsmokers. Cigarette smoke also contains carbon monoxide—a poisonous gas that can starve cells of oxygen. If you really want to do the best for your skin and you do smoke, the best thing is to cut down, or preferably give up.

caffeine

This substance is found in coffee beans, cola nuts, tea leaves, and cocoa, from which we get chocolate. It affects the central nervous system, increases the heart rate and the acidity of the stomach, and stimulates the brain, giving the illusion of a "rush" of energy. High-caffeine drinks like coffee, tea, and cola-style sodas introduce very significant levels of caffeine into the system if drunk daily. In an average cup of coffee there is a dose of approximately 125 mg of caffeine, while tea contains about 70 mg, and cola-style drinks about 55 mg. So if you drink four cups of strong coffee a day, you are taking in about 500 mg of caffeine. Caffeine places a huge burden on the liver as it tries to eliminate this toxin from the body. It also adds stress to your adrenal glands, increasing tiredness, and can contribute to premature skin aging.

Try to cut down on high-caffeine drinks to help your face, and turn to decaffeinated varieties and herbal teas as a substitute. Also, increase your water intake, aiming for the recommended daily amount of 8½ cups (see pages 100–101).

protein for muscle building

Some fashionable diets tell you to virtually eliminate protein and concentrate on carbohydrates, whereas the Atkins diet goes to the opposite extreme, encouraging a high-protein intake. The fact is that we all need a moderate amount of protein in the diet, for very important reasons. Proteins contain ingredients called amino acids, which the body must have to produce and repair tissue. There are 22 amino acids in proteins, and your body can manufacture 14 of them; the remaining 8 have to come from food.

Diets that overconcentrate on protein may not be the answer, because too much protein in the system can lead to mineral deficiency and high levels of waste products such as urea, which the kidneys have to process. Instead aim to obtain about 15 percent of your daily calorie intake from protein to achieve a moderate balance.

High-protein foods from animal sources include eggs, meat, fish, and cheese. These contain all the eight amino acids that the human body cannot make itself. However, intake of these foods needs to be moderate because some of them, especially red meat and hard cheese,

beans or lentils eaten with a grain such as brown rice will also give you the nutrients you need.

The right balance of protein in your diet will help your hair and skin to stay supple and conditioned, stop your nails from splitting, and maintain the strength of your muscles—not just in your face but all over the body. Plan your diet to include these nourishing foods and help to support your facial rejuvenation program.

Make your diet varied and interesting, and be aware of the nourishing effects of foods you put into your body. Eat with awareness!

contain high levels of saturated fat. One way to plan a balanced intake is to eat about 4 oz (115 g) of red meat, fish, or chicken three times per week, and on the days in between to choose dishes made with two eggs.

If you do not want to eat protein from animal sources, it is important to get the balance right between different vegetable sources of protein. If you look at the diet of many native American tribes, for example, they are based on a combination of corn and beans, which together constitute full protein. Baked beans on whole wheat toast (which also contains protein in the wheat germ) is a good contemporary variation on this combination. Many vegetarian dishes based around

vital nuts and seeds

If you are a vegetarian or if you simply want to add a nutrient-rich element to your diet to support your skin, it is really worth investigating nuts and seeds. They are packed with protein, vitamins, minerals, and useful fatty acids.

note

If you are allergic to nuts—as many people are these days—this section is not for you. But don't worry, there are more skin and face treats in store on the pages that follow.

nuts

Hazelnuts Sweet and tasty, they are low in fat and rich in vitamin E, and are often used in vegetarian bakes and confectionery.

Brazil nuts Creamy and delicately flavored, these nuts are a rich source of protein, B vitamins, and magnesium. They are excellent eaten alone or ground and used in nut loaves.

Almonds Delicately flavored and sweet, almonds can be bought whole, slivered, or ground. They contain protein, vitamin B2, iron, and calcium, and are delicious toasted and sprinkled over sweet or savory dishes.

Sweet chestnuts These are used throughout Europe in sweet and savory dishes. They contain more starch than other nuts and are rich in B vitamins.

Pine nuts Delicately "pine" flavored, these are a key ingredient in Italian pesto sauce, and can also be toasted and sprinkled over salads. They contain a high level of protein.

delicious three-seed garnish

Put 2 tablespoons (30 ml) each of sesame, pepitas, and sunflower seeds in a nonstick skillet. Sprinkle with organic soy sauce. Gently bring the skillet to medium heat, turning the nuts and seeds until they start to roast. Once they are browned, let the mixture cool. Enjoy the seeds as a snack or sprinkled over salads and soups.

seeds

Sesame These tiny seeds are usually pale cream in color, and are amazingly rich in vitamin B3, zinc, protein, and iron. They are made into a Middle Eastern creamy dip called sesame seed paste (tahini), and also combined with honey to make a sweetmeat called halva.

Pepitas (pumpkin) These flat round seeds with greenish skins are very crunchy and contain iron, zinc, and protein. They are delicious sprinkled over salads.

Sunflower These tiny gray seeds contain sunflower oil, which is rich in vitamin E. They are also an excellent source of B vitamins and potassium. Lightly toasted, they are very tasty sprinkled on soups or vegetable casseroles.

tip
Buy nuts and seeds in small quantities, keep them in airtight jars, and use them up quickly for maximum benefit.

super fruit boost

Fruits are packed with water, vitamins, and minerals, and they have the added advantage of tasting wonderful. Their nutrient content is very quickly absorbed by the system. Use these suggested recipes to blend fruit treats for yourself in 10 minutes that you know will benefit your skin and help your system to detoxify itself. Try one as a breakfast pick-me-up, or fit a boosting drink in at any time of the day when you feel your energy flagging. And remember—you're giving your face a real treat as well as your body!

Mango and banana milk shake

Makes 1¼ cups

Put 1 chopped banana and the flesh of 1 ripe mango into a blender with ⅔ cup of milk. Blend until smooth. This combination is full of B vitamins, beta-carotene, calcium, potassium, and magnesium.

Apple and raspberry fizz

Makes 1¼ cups

Put 1 apple, peeled, cored, and chopped, and ¼ cup of fresh raspberries into a blender with ⅔ cup of fizzy mineral water. Blend for a few seconds. This lovely fresh drink is excellent as an inner cleanser, full of vitamin C.

Pineapple and apricot milk shake

Makes 1¼ cups

Put 2 thick slices of fresh pineapple, chopped, into a blender with 5 dried apricots, chopped. Add ⅔ cup of milk, and blend until smooth. Pineapple is wonderful for the skin, because it is full of vitamin C and B vitamins, as well as minerals such as calcium, potassium, and phosphorus. Apricots are an excellent source of beta-carotene, B vitamins, and minerals such as calcium, magnesium, and zinc.

Kiwi and nectarine yog shake

Makes 1 cup

Put the chopped flesh of 1 kiwifruit and 1 ripe peeled nectarine into a blender with ¼ cup of plain yogurt and ½ cup of milk. Blend until smooth. This shake is a real nutrient treat, packed with vitamin C.

A note for vegans

You can make an excellent milk substitute from ¼ cup of slivered almonds blended with ⅔ cup of spring water, or you can use soymilk as an alternative. Soy yogurt is also available to use in the yog shake, though it has a slightly different taste.

fresh vegetable juices

You will need an electric juice extractor to make fresh vegetable juices. There are many models available, and nowadays they are not expensive to buy. The huge advantage of vegetable juices is that they deliver a really concentrated burst of vital vitamins and minerals to the body. They are also quickly absorbed, making them wonderful as a detoxifying and inner cleansing treatment, and hugely beneficial to the complexion. If you have not tried them before, you may find the taste too intense, so try diluting the fresh juices with an equal amount of spring water to start with. A glass taken before lunch is delicious, making an appetizer, which is stimulating to the taste buds.

Buy organic unsprayed vegetables where possible, to avoid any toxic chemicals. Wash them thoroughly, peel, and seed where necessary and chop them before they go in the juice extractor. Each combination makes approximately 1 cup of concentrated juice; drink it fresh on the day it is made.

Carrot and fresh ginger

Juice 3 large carrots with 1 teaspoon (5 ml) of fresh gingerroot. This combination is a delicious treat full of vitamin A, as well as the immune-enhancing and digestive-stimulating properties of ginger.

Broccoli, tomato, and red pepper

Juice 8 broccoli florets with 2 tomatoes and half a red bell pepper. This combination is full of B vitamins, beta-carotene, vitamin C, and minerals such as potassium and zinc.

Cucumber and celery

Juice 1 large cucumber with 3 stalks of celery. The juice is sweet and slightly pungent from the celery, and is an excellent detoxifying combination. It is rich in vitamin C, B vitamins, and folic acid, as well as calcium, potassium, and other vital minerals.

tips

If the vegetables are not juicing quickly, add a little bit of water into the machine as they go in to help the process along.

Don't mix fruit and vegetable juices together, as this can cause gas. The only exception is carrot and apple, which can be juiced together in equal quantities.

quality oils
why the right fats matter

With all the attention given to lowfat foods, it is interesting to note that some dietary experts are reporting seeing people who are actually fat deficient—even in a culture obsessed with weight gain and troubled with obesity. The thing about fats is that some are not helpful and some are vital, and for a glowing skin or healthy face it is necessary to include the right ones in your diet. Saturated fats, such as those found in red meat, hard cheese, and butter, can be detrimental to your heart and general health if taken in excessive amounts, whereas unsaturated fats—in the form of good-quality oils—will ease your digestion as well as improving the cellular structure of your skin, hair, and nails. The following are some excellent oils to include in your diet.

Olive oil

This oil is a staple in Mediterranean cooking, and levels of heart disease in countries such as Spain, Italy, and Portugal are low thanks to the use of this oil. Made from pressed ripe olives, the first cold pressing (extra virgin) of the fruit yields the finest quality. High in essential fatty acids, it helps to restructure dry or damaged skin and hair, and has been used cosmetically as well as in the diet for thousands of years.

Sunflower-seed oil

Rich in vitamins A, D, and E and minerals, this light and nongreasy oil is excellent for cooking and also for making salad dressings. It has a more delicate flavor.

Sesame oil

Rich and nutty, this oil is used a great deal in Chinese, Middle Eastern, and Indian cooking. It is rich in vitamin E as well as calcium, magnesium, and phosphorus. It is a staple oil in traditional Indian Ayurvedic medicine and is also extensively used for head massage or hair and skin treatments.

Try to include a total of approximately 2 tablespoons (30 ml) of these excellent oils in your cooking and salads daily; their vitamin and nutrient content will help your skin and hair to remain supple and strong, and their fat content is easily processed by the body. Your joints and digestive system will also benefit from the lubricating effect of the oils.

calcium for teeth and bones

If you eat a varied diet including some dairy products, your calcium needs are likely to be well met. If, however, your diet is strictly vegetarian or vegan, where dairy products are totally avoided, it is vital that you take in enough calcium through some of your food. If your teeth become weakened through lack of calcium, the whole cheek area and jaw can sag or give the face a sunken look, which will seriously affect the shape and structure of the face.

Calcium is needed for so many vital functions of the body.

- It promotes the growth and formation of the bones and teeth.
- It maintains the heart and muscles.
- Its presence in the tissues helps to speed up the healing process.
- It assists the passage of nutrients through cell walls.
- It helps the body to use minerals such as iron to form blood cells.

Lack of calcium can show up as premenstrual syndrome or as dehydrated skin; it can also be implicated in osteoporosis and bone or teeth deficiencies.

Fortunately, calcium is contained in many foods, from oily fish, milk, cheese, and eggs to soybeans (used to make tofu), chickpeas, and corn. Many green vegetables also contain calcium, including spinach, arugula, broccoli, kale, watercress, and salad onions, as well as young dandelion leaves in spring, which taste delicious in salads. It is also found in seaweed, which is frequently used in Japanese cooking, for example in the preparation of sushi. Almonds and sunflower seeds, as we have already seen, are also good sources of calcium.

Green vegetables should be sourced organically so that there is less risk of pesticide contamination; also the mineral content tends to be higher. Steaming or light cooking is preferable so that you obtain the maximum nutrients when you eat the vegetables.

water: a vital and simple beauty treatment

Although we are unaware of it, many of us are actually dehydrated most of the time because we do not drink enough water. Our bodies contain over 80 percent water—it is the fluid that bathes all our cells, and our kidneys use it in their constant battle to filter and clean away the toxic wastes we accumulate. Without the help of fresh water, their job is much harder, and when you load caffeine into the system via fizzy drinks and coffee, their job gets much more difficult.

In terms of your skin and face, one of the simplest and easiest commitments you can make to your health and inner cleansing is to drink 6–8 large glasses of pure spring water a day. That equals about 8½ cups. That may sound a lot, but you will be spreading it out during the day, and you will be surprised at how quickly you reach that target. You may find that it helps to choose a really beautiful glass to drink from—that way it feels as though you are drinking something more special than "just water."

For the spring water connoisseur, French mineral waters are considered to be some of the finest in the world because standards of analysis, purity, and mineral content are extremely well established there. Water from the mountain region of the Auvergne is considered to be particularly pure. There are many types to choose from, and, in France, many doctors advise drinking mineral water to help conditions such as water retention or urinary problems.

Tap water has been treated with chemicals and still contains traces of them, so it is not advised that you drink glass after glass of it. By contrast, the mineral content of pure spring water is cleansing and health-giving, which is why it is so vital to the well-being of the skin, literally plumping up the cells

tips
If you are not used to drinking a lot of water, start with a small amount and gradually increase it. If you suddenly increase your intake, you will find that most of it will be quickly eliminated, whereas if you gradually drink more, your body will have the chance to absorb it and make use of it.

facelift support treatments

Here are some lovely support treatments you can use to help you achieve the best possible effects from your facelift program. These special techniques can be used whenever you like as a way to pamper and nourish your skin, to prepare it to receive massage, or before facial exercises. They all use totally natural ingredients, so the effects on your skin will be deeply soothing. Each treatment can be done in 10 minutes, so they fit easily into a busy routine or can be used to help you unwind at the end of a busy day. Just relax and enjoy the experience.

5

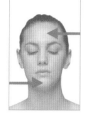

natural deep-cleansers

As well as the simple jojoba carrier cleanser mentioned earlier (see pages 72–73 and 74), there are other simple yet nourishing ways to deep-cleanse and nurture your skin. These are the kinds of preparations that were used a few generations ago when natural ingredients were the only ones to hand, and most people grew herbs in their gardens.

We consider some of the plants used here to be weeds, but our ancestors knew differently: they understood their cleansing and detoxifying effects. These days there is more of an interest in growing herbs, and fresh herbs, which are essential for these mixtures, are also available from most supermarkets, so obtaining what you need should not be difficult.

dandelion and marjoram face milk

This milk is a lovely light cleanser that is excellent for all skin types, particularly oily or mature. The dandelion leaf content also helps to lighten liver spots or freckles. Pick 4 young dandelion leaves, wash, and finely chop them, then place in a small heatproof bowl. Pick enough marjoram leaves to fill 1 tablespoon (15 ml), wash them, and add to the bowl. Pour over ⅔ cup of boiling water, place a saucer over the bowl, and leave for 5 minutes to infuse. Then strain the liquid and pour into a clean

glass bottle. Add ⅔ cup of whole milk, shake the bottle vigorously, and the face milk is ready. Keep refrigerated and use within 1 week.

honey, yogurt, and rosemary cleanser

This gentle cleanser is excellent for dry, combination, and mature skins. First, wash and measure enough fresh rosemary leaves to make 2 teaspoons (10 ml) and place them in a mug.

Add 5 tablespoons (75 ml) of boiling water and leave for 5 minutes to infuse; then strain the liquid and let it cool. In a small dish mix together 3 tablespoons (45 ml) of plain yogurt and 2 tablespoons (30 ml) of runny honey. Stir in 3 tablespoons (45 ml) of the rosemary liquid and mix to a smooth consistency. Pour into a screw-top jar and refrigerate; use within 1 week.

strawberry milk

This cleanser is so simple, and strawberries are excellent skin fresheners and toners, good for normal, oily, and mature skins. Simply blend ½ cup of milk with 4–5 washed organic strawberries; bottle and refrigerate. Use within 3 days.

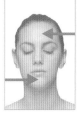

special facial scrubs

Natural face scrubs are a real treat, because as well as exfoliating (getting rid of dead skin cells on the surface) they also smooth and condition the skin, preparing it to receive a special massage treatment oil. Again, the natural ingredients are crucial—no harsh abrasives or chemicals are involved. Facial scrubs can be applied three or four times a week as a refining and cleansing treatment. Try these ideas and you will soon see good results.

azuki bean scrub

This scrub is an idea from Japan that is incredibly simple and has been used for hundreds of years for all skin types. You need some small dried red azuki beans, available from health food stores. Simply measure scant 1 cup of beans into a coffee grinder and process to a smooth powder, then store in a screw-top jar. For a scrub, place 2 tablespoons (30 ml) of this powder in a small dish, and mix it with enough water to make a smooth paste. Scrub this mixture gently over your face with small circular movements, avoiding the inner eye area. Then rinse off with warm water and pat the skin dry—it will feel incredibly soft.

oatmeal and almond scrub

This is an extremely gentle scrub that is good for all skin types, including sensitive skin. The oatmeal is cleansing and the almonds gently nourishing. In a small dish mix together 1 tablespoon (15 ml) of ground almonds with 1 tablespoon (15 ml) of fine oatmeal; add enough water to make a smooth paste. Apply

to the skin with small circular movements, avoiding the inner eye area. Rinse off with warm water and pat dry; the skin will feel smooth and very pliable.

yogurt, orange, and oatmeal scrub

This delicious scrub is good for normal, combination, and oily skins. In a dish place 2 tablespoons (30 ml) of plain yogurt, ½ teaspoon (2.5 ml) of finely grated orange rind, and 1 tablespoon (15 ml) of fine oatmeal. Mix together and apply to the face with small circular movements, avoiding the inner eye area. Rinse off and pat the skin dry—it will feel tingling and fragrant.

> ### tip
> It's best to make up a small amount of scrub each time with fresh ingredients, since the lack of preservatives means that large amounts will not keep well.

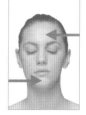

super face treats

As aromatherapists know well, a bath is a relaxing treatment in itself and a great way to unwind. As you lie in the water, steam rises to your face and your pores start to open. A great way to get more benefit from your bath is to apply a thin layer of one of these special face treats before you get in the bath, being careful always to avoid the inner eye area. While you soak in the bath, your pores will open so you will absorb all the ingredients beautifully. After the bath, wash them off with warm water, and pat the skin dry, then try some face exercises for a natural facelift effect.

sesame and honey cream

This rich liquid is marvelous for conditioning normal, mature, and combination skins. In a small dish mix together 2 tablespoons (30 ml) of sesame oil with 1 tablespoon (15 ml) of light cream and 1 tablespoon (15 ml) of runny honey. Whisk together thoroughly, pour into a screw-top jar, and refrigerate. The amount is enough for about four applications and will keep for up to 1 week.

avocado and lemon soother

This paste is a very simple treat: just mash the pulp of half an avocado to a fine paste and add 1 teaspoon (5 ml) of fresh lemon juice. This soother is excellent for normal and combination skins, because the lemon juice will lightly tone the skin while the avocado deeply nourishes it.

apricot kernel, yogurt, and geranium treat

This mixture is a richly nourishing treat for mature, normal, and even sensitive skins, making them wonderfully supple and nourished. In a small dish mix together 2 tablespoons (30 ml) of plain yogurt with 1 tablespoon (15 ml) of apricot kernel carrier oil, and add 2 drops of geranium essential oil. Whisk together then pour into a screw-top jar. This amount is enough for about four applications and will keep for up to 1 week.

special facelift programs

After all this information, you may be wondering how to get started; this section will help you do just that. Here is a series of individual facelift programs designed for all the different skin types, bringing together different combinations of the treatments and exercises shown in this book. Each program involves giving yourself a different 10-minute treatment once a day for 7 days, so that in a week your face will have 70 minutes of special care—the equivalent of a professional facial. Working a little each day means that the beneficial effects of the treatments will increase over time. There are countless ways of combining face exercises and massage techniques, but these suggestions will help you to begin.

6

dry or normal skin
facelift program

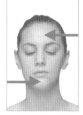

This series of treatments is designed to deeply nourish dry or normal skin as well as improve the tone of facial muscles. Notice how the exercises alternate with the facial massage sessions, culminating in the aromatherapy session with specially tailored essential oils. The treatments are best done in the evening; as well as allowing the skin to benefit during sleep, they will help to relax you. They start at the weekend, to allow you to begin when you are more relaxed. Continue with your normal beauty routine during the week, adding the exercise or treatment for the day as an extra 10 minutes of "me-time."

SATURDAY
**Simple face exercises to tone and uplift
(pages 20–21)**
Get the facial muscles moving and improve local circulation.

SUNDAY
**Deep facial rejuvenation routine
(pages 56–57)**
A nourishing treat using simple aromatherapy techniques.

MONDAY

**Face exercises for the forehead
(pages 24–25)**

Follow this routine after you have applied your night cream so that you work on smooth skin.

TUESDAY

**Eastern-style nourishing face routine
(pages 62–63)**

A glorious, delicately aromatic facial treat.

WEDNESDAY

**Face exercises for the cheeks and mouth
(pages 26–27)**

A deeper stretch for all the facial muscles.

THURSDAY

Special neck-toning routine (pages 66–67)

A luxurious special treatment using jojoba oil.

FRIDAY

**Special aromatherapy routine for dry skin
(pages 72–73)**

A beautifully balanced essential oil blend to finish your week of special care.

By the end of the week you should notice a definite improvement in skin suppleness, tone, and elasticity, and your complexion should have a lovely glow.

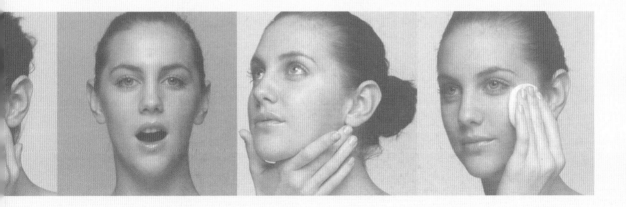

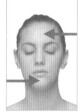

mature skin
facelift program

This program uses a wonderful variety of relaxing and toning treatments. It is designed to improve skin texture and to rejuvenate slack tissue and sagging muscles, and it starts with some concentrated exercise and massage. It is best performed in the evening as part of your facial beauty routine, adding 10 minutes each day of specialist treatment concentrated on your face. As you work your way through each element, enjoy the sensations and aromas around you.

SATURDAY
Simple Eastern head massage (pages 36–37)
Start with a deeply relaxing massage to the head and scalp to improve circulation and ease muscular tension. Remember: you can do this in the shower.

SUNDAY
Face exercises for the cheeks and mouth (pages 26–27)
Continue the exercise theme with movements and sounds designed to work the large facial muscles.

MONDAY

Deep circulation stimulating routine (pages 52–53)

Start working on the face with this deep-cleansing and nourishing treatment.

TUESDAY

Face exercises for the chin (pages 28–29)

Simple de-stressing exercises to stretch and move the lower jaw.

WEDNESDAY

Deep facial rejuvenation routine (pages 56–57)

A wonderful aromatic treat for the face combining a simple blend of essential oils in a soothing carrier oil.

THURSDAY

Sesame and honey cream facial treat (page 108)

Apply this skin treat to your face then relax in a bath with 2 drops of lavender and 2 drops of rosewood essential oil added to the water.

FRIDAY

Special aromatherapy routine for mature skin (pages 74–75)

Finish your week of special care with a luxuriously scented massage.

At the end of the week your skin should be supple and glowing.

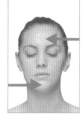

oily skin
facelift program

This series of treatments will help to maintain the natural suppleness of an oily complexion but will also help to deep-cleanse and tone the pores. Face exercises help to stimulate the circulation and ease the detoxification process. These 10-minute sessions are best performed at night for maximum benefit, and can be incorporated into your existing beauty routine. Make sure you use jojoba or apricot kernel oil as carriers for massage, as these are best suited to an oily skin.

SATURDAY
Face exercises for the forehead (pages 24–25)
Oily skin often shows deep lines in the forehead, and these exercises help to smooth them out.

SUNDAY
Basic face massage—part 1 (pages 48–49)
These simple movements help to smooth and tone the whole face.

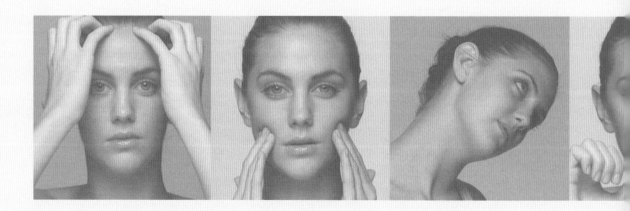

MONDAY

Face exercises for the chin (pages 28–29)

These simple movements exercise and stretch the whole neck as well as the chin.

TUESDAY

Basic face massage—part 2 (pages 50–51)

Deeper movements here really help to work the facial muscles.

WEDNESDAY

Breathe for your face (pages 32–33)

Get out into the fresh air and give your lungs, circulation, and skin the benefit of oxygen.

THURSDAY

Detoxification routine (pages 54–55)

A wonderful aromatic steam and massage treatment to deep-cleanse your skin.

FRIDAY

Special aromatherapy routine for oily skin (pages 76–77)

The beautiful essential oils, which gently cleanse and smooth the complexion, end this week of treatment.

By Friday your skin should look very supple and toned, with the pores tighter and less defined.

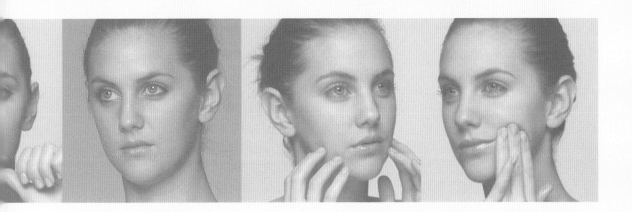

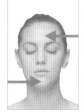

combination skin
facelift program

This series of treatments is aimed at balancing the dry and oily patches that are typical of this skin type. The Eastern face massage routines are particularly suitable because they not only work on the skin and muscles but also have an internally balancing energetic effect. Use these treatments as part of your evening beauty routine, and pay special attention to how your skin responds. If your skin tends to show varying oiliness toward the end of the menstrual cycle, this routine can be used in the week prior to menstruation to help balance the hormones.

SATURDAY
Simple face exercises to tone and uplift (pages 20–21)
Get the face toned and supple with these easy stretches.

SUNDAY
Detoxification routine (pages 54–55)
Use this lovely aromatic routine to detoxify and deep-cleanse your complexion.

MONDAY

Face exercises for the cheeks and mouth (pages 26–27)

Target key areas of the face with these deeper exercises for the muscles.

TUESDAY

Acupressure routine for facial toning (pages 58–59)

Use this specialist routine to rebalance the energy flowing through channels in your face.

WEDNESDAY

Simple Eastern head massage (pages 36–37)

Try this wonderfully simple routine with shampoo in your hair while you are in the shower.

THURSDAY

Eastern-style nourishing face routine (pages 62–63)

This lovely aromatic routine energizes and nourishes the whole face.

FRIDAY

Special aromatherapy routine for combination skin (pages 78–79)

Use these specially selected essential oils to give your skin a wonderful aromatic treat.

At the end of the week your whole complexion should be brighter and clearer, with a smoother and more supple texture.

sensitive/allergy-prone skin facelift program

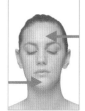

These treatments have been specially selected to care for skin that is sensitive, whether that is in response to the environment or to stress. All the work is very soothing and calming, and the aim is to support the skin as well as gently tone the facial muscles. If you think your skin is extremely sensitive, you can do all the massage treatments without essential oils; however, the suggested blends are extremely mild and should be beneficial. These treatments can be included in your general evening beauty routine.

SATURDAY

Yoga postures to improve facial circulation (pages 34–35)
Gently stretch and ease your body at the same time as nourishing your face with energy and circulation.

SUNDAY

Basic face massage—part 1 (pages 48–49)
Easy and simple moves with a plain carrier oil will softly moisturize the skin.

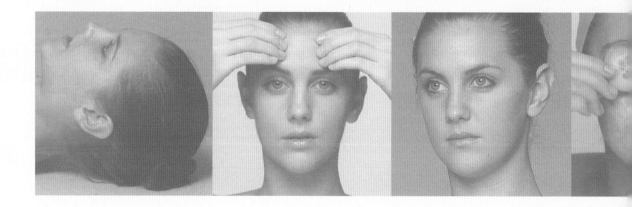

Breathe for your face (pages 32–33)
Get oxygen into your lungs and improve your skin's circulation.

TUESDAY
Deep facial cooling routine (pages 70–71)
Use this lovely cucumber mask and soothing aloe gel routine to soften and calm your skin.

WEDNESDAY
Eastern energy holds for facial vitality (pages 38–39)
Soothe and deeply relax not just your face but your whole body using these simple hand positions.

THURSDAY
Eastern-style massage to the eye area (pages 64–65)
A deeply nourishing special treat for this delicate area.

FRIDAY
Special aromatherapy routine for dry skin (pages 72–73)
Although this is a dry skin routine, the essential oils, particularly rose, also soothe and protect sensitive skin.

At the end of the week your face should feel soothed and calmed, with a supple skin texture.

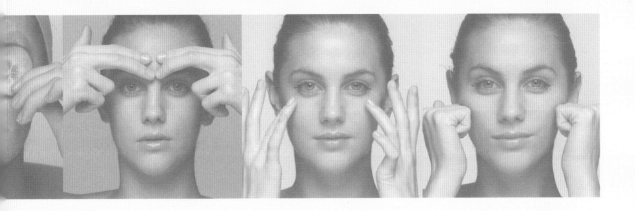

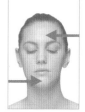

blemish-prone skin
facelift program

This program is designed to gently cleanse and support blemish-prone skin while using exercise to supply fresh circulation to the tissues to assist with detoxification. Some Eastern techniques are included to encourage energy balancing from within, as well as deep-cleansing and toning facial rejuvenation techniques for external use. The techniques will also help to de-stress and relax you, as tension can contribute to blemish outbreaks. Use the treatments in the evening as a way to help you relax and unwind.

SATURDAY
Simple face exercises to tone and uplift (pages 20–21)
Stretch and tone the facial muscles with this easy routine.

SUNDAY
Detoxification routine (pages 54–55)
This treatment gently and thoroughly deep-cleanses the skin and the deeper tissue layers.

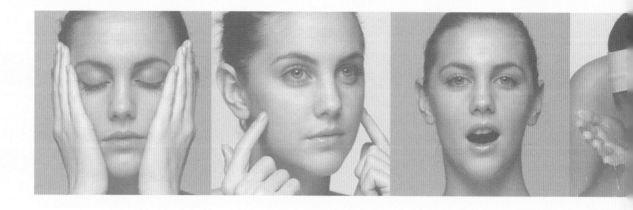

MONDAY

Face exercises for the cheeks and mouth (pages 26–27)

Deeper exercises stretch and tone the larger facial muscles.

TUESDAY

Hydrotherapy routine to deep-cleanse (pages 68–69)

This water-based treatment tones and cleanses the whole face so that the complexion tingles.

WEDNESDAY

Yoga postures to improve facial circulation (pages 34–35)

These relaxing postures help to bring fresh circulation to the whole face, so you feel revitalized.

THURSDAY

Acupressure routine for inner beauty (pages 60–61)

Special points to stimulate the energy zones in the face help to rebalance your system from within.

FRIDAY

Special aromatherapy routine for blemish-prone skin (pages 82–83)

Essential oils blended to support and heal blemish-prone skin make a luxurious final treatment.

At the end of the week your complexion should be brighter and your whole face should feel very toned.

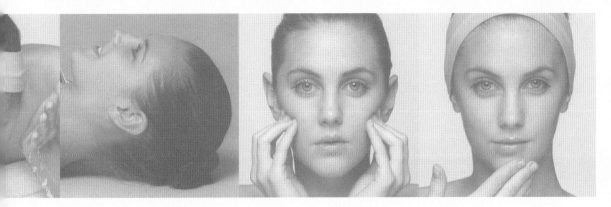

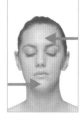

teen skin
facelift program

The teen years can play havoc with the skin, as hormones and stress levels fluctuate. This program is designed as a fun experiment for teenagers to try. You may be interested in makeup and how to achieve the "right look;" try some natural facial rejuvenation techniques to make sure that you show your best face to the world! Just 10 minutes a day for a week is easily done. Note that you can choose your aromatherapy routine depending on your skin type; not all teenagers suffer from blemishes, so select the treatment that is best for you.

SATURDAY
Simple face exercises to tone and uplift (pages 20–21)
Get into the swing of it with these simple exercises to tone and stretch the muscles.

SUNDAY
Basic face massage—part 1 (pages 48–49)
Try out these easy and simple massage strokes on clean skin.

MONDAY

Face exercises for the forehead (pages 24–25)
Wipe away stress and exercise those frontal muscles with this routine.

TUESDAY

Detoxification routine (pages 54–55)
Use this treatment to deep-cleanse and tone the skin and deeper tissues to leave the face tingling.

WEDNESDAY

Face exercises for the cheeks and mouth (pages 26–27)
Work those larger facial muscles with stretches and sounds.

THURSDAY

Hydrotherapy routine to deep-cleanse (pages 68–69)
A water treatment for soft and soothed skin, deeply cleansing and aromatic.

FRIDAY

Choose a special aromatherapy routine for your own skin type (pages 72–83)
Round off your week of 10-minute facial work with a luxurious aromatherapy treatment.

By the end of the week your skin should feel glowing and smooth, and you will feel on top of the world.

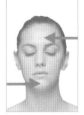

menopausal skin
facelift program

Clinically, the menopause is defined as the time when menstruation finishes, which usually occurs around the age of 50, although it varies for many women. Typical symptoms are hot flushes, changes in skin texture and suppleness, as well as mood swings and feelings of anxiety. The process of menopausal change can be supported holistically using massage and essential oils; this special program for the face will also help to de-stress and soothe the mind. Try it for a week—although you may find you want to carry on with it. Incorporate the treatments into your evening beauty routine.

SATURDAY
Face exercises for the cheeks and mouth
(pages 26–27)
Start by exercising the larger muscles in the face.

SUNDAY
Acupressure routine for inner beauty
(pages 60–61)
A really easy but energizing sequence to rebalance energy in the zones of the face.

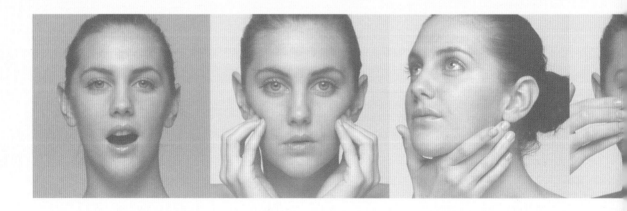

MONDAY

Special neck-toning routine (pages 66–67)
Give your neck some special attention with these sweeping movements.

TUESDAY

Deep circulation stimulating routine (pages 52–53)
A skin-softening and luxuriously aromatic treat for the face.

WEDNESDAY

Yoga postures to improve facial circulation (pages 34–35)
Stretch out and relax, and supply your face with renewed circulation.

THURSDAY

Deep facial rejuvenation routine (pages 56–57)
A richly aromatic treatment to smooth the skin and work the muscles.

FRIDAY

Eastern-style nourishing face routine (pages 62–63)
Another energetic and aromatic treatment, which will gently tone and stimulate your skin and muscles.

By the end of the week your face should appear much more glowing, with a smooth and supple skin thanks to the rich carriers and supportive essential oils in the treatments.

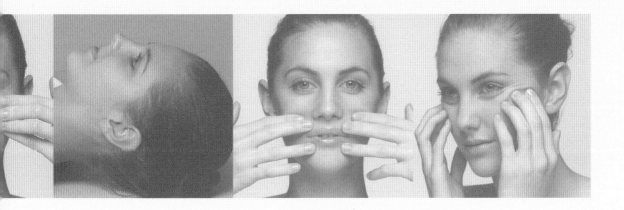

index

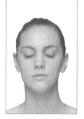